The SECRET RECORD

Michael Perkins

The

SECRET RECORD

Modern Erotic Literature

William Morrow and Company, Inc.

New York   1976

Printed in the United States of America.

1   2   3   4   5   6   7   8   9   10

Library of Congress Cataloging in Publication Data

Perkins, Michael.
    The secret record.

    Bibliography: p.
    Includes index.
    1. Erotic literature—History and criticism.   I. Title.
PN56.E7P4   809'.933'538   76-18832
ISBN 0-688-03121-8

DESIGN   CARL WEISS

To Joyce
AND TO
Leslie, Djuna, Zachary,
Leo and Jessica

Contents

INTRODUCTION

Man goes constantly in fear of
himself.
His erotic urges terrify him.

—GEORGES BATAILLE,
Death And Sensuality

THE SUBJECT of erotic literature is an area of our lives that exists within us like a separate, troubled country. Like death, sex obsesses us all in ways we often cannot define or admit, even to ourselves, but we have been trained since childhood to observe a solemn quiet on these topics, like tourists in our own souls. While people will talk freely about subjects that are of less importance to them, they are reluctant to discuss their erotic natures. Despite the unprecedented public attention given to sexuality in the past decade, for most people it is still forbidden territory, and to them, an erotic novel is still a dirty book.

Yet the function of erotic literature is to express the secret part of our lives which periodically rules us no less than money or death. By presenting erotic tumult, writers give form to emotions which are often unruly and sometimes anarchic. Their books are tentative maps—the rough cartography of explorers—which create order in the *terra incognita* of our psyches, and what can thus be circumscribed can be understood. Such writing confirms an important measure of our interior worlds and purges us of our fear of the unknown.

We read what frightens us because the work confronts our deepest suspicions about life; we agree upon an objective world we call civilization, and find in horror stories expressions of our nightmares about it. In the present, some of us go to erotic literature the way our grandparents went to *Dracula* and the tales of the Brothers Grimm: for affirmation of the creative life of chaos within ourselves. By that chaos we are reminded that we have private beings which cannot be preempted by the stern demands of the world outside us.

Erotic literature possesses a raw, innocent power which general literature has lost for many readers. It is popular writing, not yet divorced from its source in folk stories; popular, yet still socially forbidden, despite its current quasi-legal acceptance in the United States. Perhaps it is because of this power—and its underground popularity—that civilization has had so many telltale reactions to it, ranging from proscription through ridicule, feigned boredom, and uneasy condescension. Society has taken it very seriously indeed. After all, erotic writing is a threat to the conventional moral order—Dionysus calling to the demons of the unconscious—and general literature is seldom so directly threatening. The ordinary run of fiction is shelved in public libraries and ignored while society gets on with its business. Not so erotic writing. Like other branches of popular literature, it is read by people from one end of the intellectual spectrum to the other.

There is an audience for this kind of writing, perhaps larger than that for science fiction and mystery stories, but unfortunately there are not enough critics who are willing to guide readers to a deeper understanding of it. There have been some critical studies devoted to those erotic classics which have survived the centuries, but modern erotic literature, by which I mean a large number of books written from a sexual perspective and published in Europe and America in this century, has been met with silence by critics and reviewers.

An important result of this neglect of erotic literature has been that the constructive processes of public appraisal and literary criticism have not been available to it. Erotic writing is therefore peculiarly virginal, for in the absence of these reactions there are no standards by which its real achievements can be measured. Art of any kind is in one sense an argument between artist and audience, an effort by the artist to persuade his contemporaries of the truth and importance of his vision; it cannot mature without a response. Erotic writing is strong because it is read innocently and weak because its readers have no criteria by which to judge it. If it is not better one of the reasons is that society has not looked at it straightforwardly. Strother Purdy makes this point in his essay "On the Psychology of Erotic Literature."

> . . . we are forced to a partial realization of why so much erotic literature is bad: although it deals with the basis of life, censorship and guilt force it out of the normal course of life and literature, and it makes a virtue out of its handicap, strengthening rather than seeking to control and diminish its departure from verisimilitude.

What about these "dirty books" then? Are they an "important source of mythic self-knowledge," as the critic Peter Michelson believes, or are they trash, as their detractors argue? What is the difference between good and bad erotic writing and how is one to distinguish between the two?

The problem is common to every literary genre. The

formulas of popular literature may be transformed and even transcended, but if a writer succeeds in doing this, has he raised the level of the genre, or escaped it into general literature? Just as there are detective novels which affect us with the power of literature, and thousands of others which are no more than crossword puzzles, there are some erotic novels which by all standards of literary judgment are works of art. This should seem self-evident to the informed, unbiased reader, but most people are unable to approach erotic literature without a personal bias based on their attitude toward its subject matter. Yet while it is not necessarily true that understanding produces sympathy, it is obvious that intolerance inhibits understanding.

Still worse for attaining a broader perspective on the field is the attitude that grants erotic literature its occasional masterpiece while scorning the genre from which they arise. Exceptional work may be found in every genre, but before the masterpieces of erotic literature can be accurately assessed, it will be necessary for the discriminating reader to accept the murky Mississippi from which they flow as a legitimate waterway.

Europeans poke fun at Americans writing about sex; we approach the subject too piously, they say. They're probably right. There is something in our souls—is it still that durable Puritan awareness of sin?—which makes it necessary for us to treat sex like thin ice, likely to crack beneath us. We take our sex as seriously as we used to take our work, constantly trying to improve it, tinkering with it, justifying it, unable to leave it alone to nourish us. Being American, I agree that sex is no laughing matter. Although I believe that joy is one of the synonyms of sex, and that erotic writing lends itself to a comic approach, laughter is often the most effective obstacle to sexual arousal. Despite this, humor, which includes the grotesque, the awkward, and the embarrassing occasion in bed, has been a fertile source of themes in erotic fiction.

What are some of the other themes—as opposed to the formulas—of erotic literature? Fantasy has been an important and pervasive element in the genre. Few of us will ever murder someone, travel to Mars, punch cows on the open range, or satisfy a dozen beautiful women at an orgy; but we can live these experiences vicariously. Obviously one of the attractions of fiction is that it enables us to live a thousand lives we wouldn't have the courage, time, or inclination for in reality; erotic fiction dramatically increases the number of vicarious experiences available to us. We all have sex lives, but few of us are murderers or space travelers. In most instances however, the themes of erotic writing are the familiar themes of mainstream writing, among them innocence and its loss; degradation and redemption; freedom and enslavement; desire and its consequences; and the transcendence of the ego.

One of the functions of literature, and especially popular literature, is to reflect and report upon the passions of the day. Presently, when sex occupies so prominent a place in our cultural life, it doesn't seem outrageous to suggest that erotic writing may be the popular literature that most accurately mirrors a large part of contemporary life, a secret record, so to speak, of our secret lives. In any event, thinking about sexuality has undergone such a rapid change in the past decade that its literature has become progressively acceptable to large numbers of people, particularly the young, who read erotic writing as much for entertainment and the confirmation of their own beliefs and lifestyles as for titillation. People have seen that the insights of Freud and the discoveries of sexual research since Freud can hardly be applied by a literature which ignores sexuality.

These are some of the arguments for an intelligent reading of erotic literature and for its acceptance as a legitimate genre of writing, but the most important is pleasure. Which is to say: what is wrong with reading a book for the purpose of both physical and mental stimulation? And what is aroused in us by a reading of the classics but the very basic emotions of pity, sympathy, love, and terror? Why do we forbid ourselves sexual arousal when we read?

Eros is, in the classical sense, one of the first impulses of all literature. Poets feel a connection with eros both historical and personal, which may be why so many of them have contributed to modern erotic writing. The connection between poets and erotic writing has been a productive one. The interest of poets in exploring the potential of this genre of fiction coincided with a period in history when legal and market conditions were right. When the 1966 U.S. Supreme Court decision on pornography made possible the publication of explicitly erotic novels, the demand for writers by publishers in the field was so great there were ample opportunities for anyone who could write a sentence. Most of these publishers appeared from nowhere, with no experience or interest in publishing beyond the money to be made during a boom, and they protected themselves by insisting on formula hackwork designed to appeal to the widest audience; but a few had the imagination—or the indifference—to commission work by young writers curious and open about the form and in need of the relatively small fees that were being paid.

Their encounters with a form as rigid in some ways as the Japanese *haiku* produced variations, viewpoints, and styles they could only have arrived at in erotic fiction. Perhaps that is why their novels are often more exciting than other areas of contemporary literary experimentation: this tension between tradition and formula and the freedom to work up to the limits of one's erotic imagination. Of course for every good erotic novel, there are a thousand failures; nevertheless, a serious assessment of the achievements of the genre is long past due.

It may be useful to list at the start what this book is, and what it is not; to define, and to note some intentions.

In the context of this book, erotic literature means any imaginative writing that is mainly about sexuality. Beyond this simple definition lie too many complications not relevant to our purposes here. The adjective *erotic* pertains to the sexual passions; the words *obscene* or *pornographic* are so laden with legal connotations that they will be used as little as possible. Let lawyers quibble and writers publish. This book is not a history of eroticism, a history of censorship, or an apologia for dirty books. Instead it is what used to be called an appreciation—of the genre, and of certain writers in it. It is also a practical literary tour through previously uncharted territory, the erotic literature of this century. Finally, it is an attempt to persuade readers that there is a secret literature under their noses worthy of intelligent attention and respect.

It would be unnatural if the reader, after going this far, did not wonder for a moment about the author's own point of view. I believe that sexuality is fully as important a subject for literature as is war, death, or the struggle to survive and enjoy the time between our beginnings and our common end. I see the print of eros on every page, and in every life.

The SECRET RECORD

I

DIONYSIAN LITERATURE

THE EROTIC IMPULSE has been a lively and vital force in literature since the beginning of recorded history. As soon as man began to write things down, he wrote about the awesome role of sexuality in his life. These writings can be traced back as far as the Sumerian civilization, to love songs chanted at the symbolic marriage of the king to a priestess of Inanna, goddess of love and reproduction. For thousands of years eros had an honored place in the official writings of civilization after civilization.

But these were simple love songs. It isn't until we turn

to the legends of ancient Greece that sexuality enters literature as a disruptive, demonic force. At the beginning of the
last millennium B.C., Thracians brought the cult of the
wine god Dionysus to Greece.

Dionysus was the best loved son of Zeus. He was torn
to pieces by jealous gods and eaten, but his heart was saved,
and from it his father was able to resurrect him. The cult
of Dionysus was an ecstatic, sexual religion of wide popularity. Its most famous adherents were Greek women who
left their homes in the spring to roam the mountains. There,
for days at a time, they danced, made love, and drank until
they had worked themselves into such a frenzied state they
were able to make a live sacrifice of an animal, a child, or
a man. Tearing it limb from limb as Dionysus had been
torn, they drank its blood and ate its flesh in the belief that
thereby they were communing with their god.

The mortal incarnation of Dionysus dressed in animal
skins, smeared his face with wine dregs, and wore a large
artificial phallus as the symbol of his godhood. (Dionysus'
son was Priapus, god of procreation, whose symbol was an
erect penis.) The women who followed him were called
either maenads—mad women—or Bacchoi. They dressed in
fawn skins, and were possessed of a fierce strength able to
overcome any human resistance, an insatiable sexuality, and
an ability to commune directly with wild things. The rites
they practiced would be proscribed if they occurred anywhere in the modern world, but they are recalled in two
branches of literature: the drama and erotic writing. With
the passage of time, almost every disruptive impulse en-
countered in literature comes under the intellectual control
of form, but the wine-smeared visage of Dionysus still leers
up at us from the pages of the contemporary erotic novel.

The connection between eros and poetry to which I
will refer often in these pages begins with Dionysus. The
two share like a radiant nimbus the sense of ecstatic celebra-

tion of the Dionysian festivals. They first illuminate in the light of joy before they begin to frighten us.

We will return to this connection, but now let us follow the Dionysian influence where it leads us in literature. Starting out on foot in the clear Greek light with Dionysus as our guide dancing somewhere ahead of us, we come upon a white stone amphitheater where Euripides' tragedy *The Bacchae* is being recited. *The Bacchae* draws upon the legend of Dionysus for its plot only so that Euripides may warn against the dangers of religious mania, but the hymns he writes to Dionysus recreate the passionate emotions of Dionysian festivals. *The Bacchae* is the first well-known instance of the Dionysian influence on literature, but that influence is also found throughout Greek tragedy and comedy. It becomes specifically sexual in Aristophanes' *Lysistrata*, with its story of wives withholding sex until their warrior husbands make peace, and there are sexual overtones in a number of other classical plays.

The Dionysian influence is also seen in Greek lyric poetry, particularly the songs of Sappho of Lesbos. Although her work has survived only in evocative fragments, in each Sapphic fragment we can still hear the husky voice of a celebrant of eros. Her lyrics were equalled by those collected in the *Greek Anthology*, and one of the poets whose work is found there, Diogenes Laertius, even speaks of the "forecasting brute with the long slimy tongue," a prophetic reference to Dionysus.

When Dionysus crossed the Mediterranean to Italy, the Romans changed his name to Bacchus, but his influence shows no sign of diminishment in the work of Ovid, Petronius, Martial, Juvenal, and Catullus. In *Amores*, or the *Art of Love*, we find Ovid giving advice to the man who wants to win a mistress on how to get and hold her, and to the mistress on how to satisfy her lover. Even in that relatively tolerant age Ovid found himself exiled for his boldness of speech, although his lines are mild compared to the frankly erotic language of Petronius Arbiter. The series of fragments which make up his *Satyricon* are filled with stories about homosexuals, cheating lovers, and husbands who double as pimps.

Catullus, along with Propertius the greatest of Roman love poets, wrote lyrics which in modern translations reveal a frankness about fellatio and anal sex—among the other courses of love—as uncompromising as any fiction we read today. Martial and Juvenal, cynical spectators of the excesses of first-century Rome, described in biting, satirical verse their pungent reactions to it. Their lines are still capable of arousing the censor's wrath when translated into modern idioms. This is a catamite in Juvenal's *Satires:* "Penetration from the rear/is only part of my unfortunate story." Or Martial, in one of his mocking sexual epigrams: "When you hear clapping from the baths,/Maron's mighty cock is sure to be the cause."

The point has been made before, by historians, scholarly writers, and translators: the great Greek and Roman poets wrote freely about the sexual activities of their times, using language which most people today would find obscene. This has hardly been a well-kept secret in this century, but it was for a thousand years to people who had no Greek or Latin and had to depend upon timid translations. For those unfamiliar with classical literature, a reminder that erotic literature doesn't begin with *Fanny Hill* should suffice. Erotic literature began in hymns to gods of reproduction and eros, moved from Greek drama to Roman poetry, and even makes an appearance in the *Bible* and medieval literature. Erotic writing, far from being the illegitimate bastard of literature, can lay claim to an illustrious ancestry.

It may be argued that the intention of the Roman poets when they described sexuality was different from the intention of modern erotic writers. Obviously there are differences, of execution as well as intention. Probably the most basic difference is historical. How a work is going to be received, and by what audience, creates an attitude which may determine a writer's feeling of freedom about his work. Juvenal, for instance, is generally regarded as a moralist. He satirized the sexuality of his time because it was part of the decadence he wanted to flay in his verse. Ovid, on the other hand, wrote to amuse as well as to instruct. In the modern world morality, amusement, and instruction have not been considered sufficient justification for reading erotic writing.

In the Middle Ages erotic writing suffered the neglect of literature in general. It was severely curtailed, showing up mostly in low verse, jokes, and riddles. Apparently one of the favorite targets of doggerel writers was clerical immorality; these same lascivious monks were also the caretakers of ancient literature. It is fascinating to speculate on the erotic books that were lost because of them.

In the fourteenth century, Christian holidays still incorporated the old pagan fertility rites, and two masterpieces—Boccaccio's *Decameron* and Chaucer's *Canterbury Tales*—appeared, to the delight of educated, tolerant readers. Although neither book may be called erotic, they both glow with the clear light of sexuality. As David Loth observes in *The Erotic In Literature,* they are the ancestors of the modern bedroom farce. They evoke laughter at the expense of human sexual foibles more than they arouse sexual feelings.

By the time of the Renaissance erotic writing began to be treated as something special and perhaps scandalous. It wasn't yet forbidden, but the influence of the predominant Judaeo-Christian code was beginning to manifest itself in hypocrisy. Sexual realities didn't change, but writing about them had to become more cautious. The Dionysian influence in literature was still strong, but it went masked.

Yet despite the restrictive codes which affected sexual behavior, despite the strict censorship of political, scientific, and theological writing, the Dionysian spirit contributed to the lusty flavor of Elizabethan writing, notably in Shakespeare's plays. Certainly no one would claim that Shakespeare was a particularly erotic writer (except possibly Thomas Bowdler, who produced a "family Shakespeare" by cutting every sexual reference from the plays), but when he felt the situation was appropriate he wrote freely.

There is a word not much used these days which defines the Dionysian influence in Renaissance writing. It is *ribald*, meaning obscene, irreverent, scurrilous. It has a lighter connotation than *obscene*, or *pornographic*, implying a tolerance of sex in writing if used amusingly. Most of the literature of the English Restoration, especially the plays of William Congreve, John Dryden, and William Wycherley are ribald rather than erotic. The exception was a play called *Sodom, or The Quintessence of Debauchery* by John Wilmot, the Earl of Rochester. But before we meet Rochester, the English precursor of the Marquis de Sade, chronology requires a glance at some of the major erotic writings of France, Italy, and China.

The Dialogues of Luisa Sigea by Nicolas Chorier appeared in France around 1660. It was the *Joy of Sex* of its time, one of the first sex manuals, although it was fiction and cast in the form of a dialogue between women. It was written to counteract the prevailing anti-sex attitude of what was permissible for ladies of the time, and in it women talk to women about the arts of love with a directness which exceeded the limits of ribaldry.

> They call the extreme part of the penis, being oblong, head; if thou squeezedst it between the tips of thy fingers, far from doing it the slightest harm, thou wouldst cause the most pleasing sensation. . . .

The dialogue form remained popular for hundreds of years; one of the most famous French erotic novels, *A Lady of Quality*, attributed to Crébillon le Fils, is set in the form of a dialogue. It is more stylistically graceful than *Luisa Sigea*, and less of a sex manual, comparable to Choderlos de Laclos' epistolary novel of jaded passion, *Dangerous Acquaintances*.

Dialogue was used expertly in the sixteenth century by Pietro Aretino, whose *Sonnets*, published in 1527, is sometimes mistakenly considered the first erotic book in the western world. His *Harlot's Dialogues* between an anxious mother and her more experienced friend demonstrate that Renaissance Italy was as preoccupied with the sexual education of young girls as France.

There is a vast body of Oriental erotic literature as worthy of note as the European, but its influence on modern erotic literature is negligible, so we will simply note one of its classics. The *Chin P'ing Mei* appeared in China at about the same time as *A Lady of Quality* and *The Harlot's Dialogues* appeared in Europe. It is a sixteen-hundred-page novel from which the erotic chapters have been excerpted by modern translators and published separately as either *House of Joy* or *The Love Pagoda*, depending upon the publisher. This novel is as famous as the *Jou Pou Tuan*, and holds the reader's interest for two reasons: its energetic celebration of sexuality, even of those acts which are labeled abnormal, and the dominant idea that the sexually wicked are rewarded and the innocent are punished which foreshadows Sade's treatment of the same idea in *Justine*.

The tradition upon which modern erotic novelists draw is English and French for the most part, and until the Earl of Rochester published his *Sodom* in 1684 there hadn't been a writer in England whose treatment of eros could be called more than ribald. Rochester was the first English writer to take the subject of sex as seriously and obsessively as modern authors do.

Rochester's biography is as outrageous as his erotic verse. He died at the age of thirty-three in 1680 after a life spent whoring and drinking, playing practical jokes, satirizing the court of Charles II, and attempting to put into practice what he wrote. In this he resembles Sade, who lived much longer—perhaps because he spent so much time in prison or the madhouse with a cell door between him and temptation. The importance of both Rochester and Sade to us is that—aside from a certain correspondence between their lives—they both composed erotic masterpieces based on ideas they had attempted to test in reality; in addition, both of them for the first time wrote what modern jurists would be forced to call pornography.

There are major differences between the two men, however. Rochester's erotic verse, and particularly his *Sodom,* was intended to be satirical and amusing, although it contained a cutting edge. He was after all, a court jester who tried the patience of a notably tolerant king, and when he was finally banished from the court it was because of his irreverent diatribes, not because of his ideas. Sade, by contrast, considered himself a serious philosopher unjustly prevented from staging some of his grandest conceptions.

Placed next to any of Sade's most famous books, *Sodom* is likely to look like no more than controversial entertainment. Its orgiastic plot, furthered by characters with names like Fuckadilla, Cuntigratia and Buggeranthos, might cause a sensation on Broadway, but it is doubtful if an audience would flee in horror from it. With its anti-Puritan theme it might even be accepted as a piece of bold theater. By contrast, a theatrical presentation of Sade's *Philosophy in the Bedroom* would cause the commitment of everyone involved to a modern Charenton.

Typical of *Sodom* are these stage directions at the end of the second act:

> They dance six naked men and women, the men doing obedience to the women's cunts, kissing and touching them often, the women in like manner to the men's Pricks, kissing and dandling their Codds, and then fall to fucking, after which the women sigh and the men look simple and so sneak off.

Rochester may claim the honor of being the first erotic writer in English whom legal minds would find pornographic, but his career was but a prelude to that of the thinker who was put in an insane asylum by his family at the age of sixty-four because—as the police put it—he was in a state of "constant licentious insanity."

Sade is the first philosopher of eroticism, the first writer who frightens us because of the nature of his sexual visions. His ideas are certainly more complex and disturbing than the popular image of him as a sexual Dracula suggests. But for the details of Sade's constructed life, for an interpretation of his major texts, more thorough studies are required; let us just look briefly at some of the reasons why he is such an important figure in the history of erotic literature. It is as if Dionysus in his darkest mood had surfaced in the person of an eighteenth-century French nobleman.

Sade did not censor his perceptions of the power and importance of sexuality. Instead, he developed an intellectual framework for their expression. He believed that he should be allowed to do as he wished sexually without regard for the feelings or physical pain of others, and he believed this strongly enough to put his ideas into practice. This may make him a madman, or a visionary, but, he cannot be dismissed as a pornographer; he will not go away. He was obsessively sincere about what he wrote, which is what we find most frightening.

He imagined scenes reminiscent of what took place during the Dionysian festivals two thousand years before him. He imagined sex as religion, and every worshipper a god; whippings, torture, every human orifice at once a temple and a desecration. The human was the measure of everything. Nothing existed outside the individual ego.

Modern erotic literature properly begins with Sade, in *Justine, Juliette,* and the *Philosophy in the Bedroom.* Few erotic novelists since him have bothered to buttress their narratives with philosophical supports, but his influence is evident throughout the history of the genre. If any thinker in history reminds us of the imperatives of eros, it is Sade, who first proclaimed the selfish majesty of the genitals.

After Sade, the Dionysian influence in literature began to be determined by the conditions of the literary marketplace. Because of social and legal sanctions no writer would undertake to write new songs and narratives for the god unless he was well paid. John Cleland, author of *Memoirs of a Woman of Pleasure,* or *Fanny Hill,* was the first commercial erotic writer, and he was arrested for his authorship of that chaste classic of a whore's progress in London—although his punishment was a mere slap on the wrist followed by the granting of a pension. *Fanny Hill* was published in London in 1749; at approximately the same time, three classics of English literature appeared: Henry Fielding's *Tom Jones,* Samuel Richardson's *Clarissa,* and Tobias Smollett's *Roderick Random.* In the context of these novels *Fanny Hill* may be seen with a more dispassionate eye than is possible when it is viewed as popular pornography. Cleland's book is explicitly erotic (although not one four-letter word sullies his story) in its narrative of a young girl's sexual adventures in Georgian London, but, as in *Clarissa,* love rises above sex and justifies her amorous activities. Like Fielding and Richardson, Cleland was a sentimental, romantic writer, but unlike them he chose to be explicitly erotic rather than bawdily suggestive. He is a minor talent and they are major figures, but if they had been as honest in their treatment of sexuality, the history of erotic literature might have been different.

The major nineteenth-century novelists who came after Richardson and Fielding did not write honestly about sexuality. Their references to it are always oblique. The Dionysian element in the mainstream of literature had been forced underground. *Fanny Hill* marks the beginning of the commercial exploitation of eros, and the end of the first stage of Dionysian literature.

II

VICTORIAN EROTICA

IT MUST SEEM paradoxical to people unfamiliar with erotic literature that although Queen Victoria's reign in England defined the limits of human prudery—it was a time when even piano legs were covered with ruffles for modesty's sake— Victorian erotica is the most mechanically licentious in the history of erotic writing. In considering this disparity, however, we must not forget that the Dionysian element—forced from its once prominent place in mainstream literature—was now served by commercial, obsessive writers, those we have been calling pornographers for the past hundred years.

The collection of Victorian erotica is so vast it might fill an anteroom in Buckingham Palace, but the few books of any real interest would fit on one small shelf. The erotic writing of the time is so uniform in theme and execution that sketches of a half-dozen books will suffice for an assessment of its position in the history of the genre. Steven Marcus, in his brilliant and indispensable study of Victorian erotica, *The Other Victorians* (1966), rightfully criticizes its obsessive repetitiousness, but then proceeds to make assumptions about erotic writing in general as if the genre began and ended in the Victorian era.

A pornographic work of fiction characteristically develops by unremitting repetition and minute mechanical variation—the words that may describe this process are again, again, again, and more, more, more.

To argue that Victorian erotica is not of value because of its repetitiousness is one thing, but to include all erotic writing in this argument is quite another. Any fool can see that the problem with Victorian erotica—or indeed, modern erotica done by a formula—is its tiresome monotony. But Marcus doesn't limit his criticism to the repetitious plot action of Victorian writing. What he seems to be implying is that every "pornographic work of fiction" is flawed because it must describe the repetitious nature of the sexual act itself. This is like arguing that biography is an inferior literary form because everyone is born, lives a life, and dies. The facts of anyone's life are basically the same to the statistician, but the interpretation of a particular groan makes all the difference in understanding. One of the characteristics of any of our highest moments is that they are repetitious—or we would like them to be. Any satisfying experience calls for repetition—again, again, more, more—even to excess. Nevertheless, although it is necessary to take issue with some of Marcus' generalizations, *The Other Victorians* remains the only worthwhile critical study of Victorian erotica.

Bearing in mind that the Victorian era was not only prudish but socially enlightened, it is shocking to come upon a literature of sexuality whose most prominent features are flagellation and the molestation of children. Marcus has coined a word, pornotopia—"that vision which regards all of human experience as a series of exclusively sexual events or conveniences"—that provides an excellent starting point for a summary of erotic writing in the nineteenth century. Surely the most famous autobiography of the time, *My Secret Life*, is pornotopian. In its American edition (1966) *My Secret Life* runs to several thousand pages, and on each page the autobiographer—who calls himself Walter—describes one or more sexual encounters. After a few hundred pages of this, even the most receptive reader must stop and wonder about Walter's single-mindedness. *My Secret Life* is the *reductio ad absurdum* of the pornotopian vision.

Fortunately it is an anomaly in the history of erotic literature. It sums up the repetitious obsessiveness of the era, and as far as we know it is fact and not fiction. It is a record rather than a celebration of the erotic impulse, and despite Marcus' observation that Victorian erotic fiction liked to present itself as factual, there is a gulf between Walter's salacious bookkeeping and the sometimes artful fantasizing found in erotica of the period.

Before looking at these period pieces of the erotic imagination however, let us see what happened to the Dionysian influence. Dionysus is an opponent of order, idealism, and progress, the ideals of the era. He was banished by it, and his literature forbidden, only to turn up for sale in London's Holywell Street, where in 1834 the Society for the Suppression of Vice found fifty-seven shops engaged in the sale of pornography. The public had rejected honest Dionysian writing, but it still desired its forbidden books. The Dionysian impulse had turned inward, and erotic writing was left to pornotopians.

Typical of what they wrote is *The Pearl*. It was the underground journal of sex for Victorian London from July, 1879 to December, 1880, the *Screw* magazine of the times. Instead of news, *The Pearl* published novels, short stories, ballads, and poems. One of these novels, *Miss Coote's Confession, or the Voluptuous Experiences of an Old Maid*, demonstrates the Victorian interest in flagellation:

> . . . my poor bottom is beginning to be finely pickled, and I can feel the blood trickling down my legs inside my drawers.

Another novel published in *The Pearl*, *My Grandmother's Tale, or May's Account of Her Introduction to the Art of Love* shows an interest in young girls:

> "You have a dear little cunt, very fat and plump. But I wonder you have much hair on it. How old are you, Nina?"
> "Just fifteen, sir."

A few lines are sufficient to illustrate the recurring themes of Victorian erotica. There was something dammed up which found expression in novels that ignored the demands of reality, breaking the continuity between real life and its fictional representation. Nowadays it is expected that much of erotic writing will involve the transcription of personal fantasies, a tendency we can trace back to the Victorian period.

Naturally writing that finds no acceptable niche within the real world is going to be artificial, narcissistic, and unrealistic, but each age has its own erotic fantasies. In our age they are closer to historical realities than in Victorian England, but even then there was a connection between erotic fantasy and history. England was at the height of her imperialist phase in India and the Mediterranean when two of the most famous novels of the Victorian age were published: *A Night in a Moorish Harem* and *Venus in India*. People at home were familiar with stories told them by colonial relatives and friends of a less restricted sexuality to the south and consequently were receptive to erotic fantasies placed in exotic foreign locales.

A Night in a Moorish Harem is written with that florid Victorian fluidity of style which tastes sugary to the modern palate. It concerns a young naval officer named Lord George Herbert—supposedly the handsomest man in England—whose ship is anchored off Morocco. He goes sailing, falls asleep in his small boat, and when he awakens finds that his boat has drifted near a harem of nine women. Their master is away, so our hero undertakes to satisfy their desires all by himself. Of course his sexual prowess is nothing short of marvelous; it must be, to fulfill the age-old male fantasy of a personal harem. To flesh out the slim premise of the novel, each harem woman tells Lord George of her previous *amours*. (Incidentally this device, a woman telling a man of her past sexual experience in order to titillate him, is repeated over and over in erotic literature.) After hearing one such story, Lord George describes his reaction:

> My crest went plunging in, tore through the curtain of her virginity and rammed against her pregnant womb. 'Allah! Allah!' she moaned, tossing her arms wildly upward and rolling her eyes toward heaven. Whether her pain or her pleasure was most exquisite I do not know, but my whole being seemed to center in my loins and gush into the beautiful Moor. Then I sank prostrate and exhausted on her bosom with every desire gratified.

It is explained in the text how a virgin may become pregnant, but nowhere are euphemisms like "crest" for the penis justified. Victorian prudery had a long reach, capable of influencing even the language of its forbidden books. It also indicates that erotic writers weren't entirely out of touch with historical reality. Despite the strong element of fantasy in their books, they managed to reflect some of the social attitudes of their time about sexuality. *A Night in a*

Moorish Harem is sticky with euphemisms. Sexual histories are substituted for characterization, the plot is advanced solely by Lord George's amazing prowess, and romance veils all.

Venus in India by Captain Charles Devereaux is even more of a tribute to the conventions of the age. It is predictably repetitious, euphemistically sweetened, and exotic; but it contains maidens whose protests against sex (although they eventually surrender to passion) are as gushily sincere as any in the popular romantic novels of the period.

The indefatigable hero of *Venus in India* is once again a military officer left stranded with some beautiful maidens; he is a Victorian gentleman stationed in India during the war with the Afghans. Captain Devereaux gets involved with a married woman whose husband is off at the front in the first story of the novel; in the second story, it is the teenaged daughters of his commanding officer who drain his manly energy. (The Victorian word for semen was "spend"; Marcus has pointed out the connection between sex and money this word represents, but not its other Victorian meaning of the expenditure of limited energies.)

Even as a curiosity, without its erotic scenes *Venus in India* is of little interest. With the core of sex provided by the author it becomes a much more significant document. It provides glimpses of Victorian realities, mostly the sexual, of course, as in this indictment of the Victorian wife's attitude towards sex:

> For my dearest wife, gentle reader, was the life of passion; she was not one of those who coldly submit to their husband's caresses because it is their duty to do so, a duty however not to be done with pleasure or joyfully, but more as a species of penance! No! With her it was not, "Ah! no! let me sleep tonight, dear. I did it twice last night, and I really don't think you can want it again. You should be more chaste, and not try me as if I were your toy and plaything. No! Take your hand away! Do leave my nightdress alone! I declare it

is quite indecent the way you are behaving!" and so forth, until, worn out with her husband's pertinacity, she thinks the shortest way, after all, will be to let him have his way, and so grudgingly allows her cold slit to be uncovered, unwillingly opens her ungracious thighs, and lies a passionless log, insensible to her husband's endeavors to strike a spark of pleasure from her icy charms. . . .

Even the reader who has but a casual acquaintance with Victorian fiction will recognize the conventions and coy usages in this passage, from "gentle reader" through the cry of chastity: "no, no, a thousand times no!" Here in one paragraph is captured the traditional expression of Victorian anti-sexuality in its own flowery language. If only Dickens had written it!

Captain Devereaux rejects the pleas of chastity for a more pleasing sensuality among women who in an exotic locale may ignore convention, but, even with them, he is never less than a gentleman. He adheres to prudish mores even as his crest rises in his trousers.

Flossie, sometimes attributed to the poet Algernon Charles Swinburne (though without the slightest evidence for the claim) is the *Deep Throat* of the Victorian era. It is briefer and less floridly written than most Victorian erotica. It has the virtue, rare in these novels, of coming directly to the point. Captain Archer, the narrator of the novel, is an experienced man of thirty-five when he meets fifteen-year-old Flossie while strolling in Piccadilly. He is immediately struck by the size of her breasts, and is happy when he receives a note from her guardian, Miss Eva Letchford, encouraging him to become Flossie's companion because the girl has fallen in love with him. But Flossie has promised Miss Letchford that her hymen will remain intact. Sexual activity will have to be limited to fellatio and cunnilingus—"gamahuching" as the Victorians called oral sex—but as Flossie and Captain Archer practice them, these activities are never limited.

Flossie is notable for its concentration on oral-genital activities, and its heroine's youth, as well as its direct, uncluttered language, but it is no more than a piece of entertaining fluff —no small achievement however, for so solemn a time.

Steven Marcus has dealt extensively with four other Victorian erotic novels worth mentioning, as well as the primary reference book in the field, Henry Spencer Ashbee's *Index Librorum Prohibitorum,* an annotated bibliography of Victorian erotica published under the pseudonym of Pisanus Fraxi. Since it would be pointless to retrace the same ground Marcus has covered so thoroughly, I will simply refer the interested reader to his analyses of some famous Victorian erotica: *The Lustful Turk, Rosa Fielding, or, A Victim of Lust, The Amatory Experiences of a Surgeon,* and *Randiana.* These novels are used by Marcus in *The Other Victorians* to illustrate his conception of pornotopia. Once again his specific complaints about these books—that they are mechanical and repetitious—are on target, but they do not justify general conclusions like the following:

> Pornography is, after all, nothing more than a representation of the fantasies of infantile sexual life, as these fantasies are edited and reorganized in the masturbatory daydreams of adolescence. . . .

Now this conclusion may be true of the four novels Marcus has discussed, or indeed, even of most Victorian erotica; but the distinction that must be made is that Victorian erotic writing is anomalous in the history of the genre. Neither before the nineteenth century nor after it is erotic literature so deadening and so unrealistic, so reduced to mechanical fantasies. When the Dionysian element in literature is accorded its rightful place by a society, it is a complex mixture of reality and fantasy; only when it is forced underground does it fit Marcus' description. He is misleading when he judges pornography at its worst. Repression was the basis of Victorian civilization; it is not the psychology likely to produce a healthy erotic literature.

Having glanced so cursorily (the subject warrants no more attention from the general reader) at some Victorian erotica, it seems appropriate to conclude with a quotation from Ashbee's *Index Librorum Prohibitorum*. First published in 1877, it remains the one book which covers the field sympathetically and thoroughly. Ashbee writes:

> I hold that for the historian or the psychologist, these [erotic] books, whether in accordance with, or contrary to the prejudices and tendencies of the age, must be taken into account as well as, if in preference to those in many other and better cultivated fields of literature. . . .
> I maintain that no product of the human brain should be ignored, entirely disregarded, or allowed to become utterly lost; for every writing, however trifling or insignificant it may seem, has a value for the *true* student, in estimating the individual who wrote it, or the period in which it was produced.

Ashbee's guide to Victorian erotica follows these principles to the letter. A glance at its plot descriptions and quotations may tell you more than you want to know about Victorian psychology.

> EXHIBITION OF FEMALE FLAGELLANTS, in the Modest & Incontinent World, Proving from indubitable facts that a number of Ladies take a secret Pleasure in whipping their own, and Children committed to their care, and that their Passion for exercising and feeling the Pleasure of a Birch-Rod, from objects of their Choice of both sexes, is to the full as Predominant as that of mankind.

It has become an axiom of popular psychology that the repression of pleasure equals the expression of cruelty to the same intensity, and Ashbee's book bears witness to its truth. In Victorian times rigid repression twisted sexuality into a small and private violence which manifested itself in the rod. But the rod would come to seem an amusement next to the violence of the twentieth century.

In the nineteenth century began the mechanization of people, who became replaceable parts in the factories of progress. Victorian erotica mirrors this condition, and we can see in its scenes of whippings a hint of worse violence to come, as people reacted to the suppression of their erotic natures. A century later, we are just beginning to reassert our rights as sensitive flesh, and to listen once again for the songs of Dionysus rather than the cries of Dionysian destructiveness.

III

THE INNOCENCE OF EVIL

> Eroticism is different from animal
> sexuality in that for a man aroused
> clear images surge up with the dis-
> tinctness of objects; eroticism is the
> activity of a conscious being.
>
> —GEORGES BATAILLE

IF THE EROTIC literature of a nation may be said to reveal its sexual imagination, sexuality in Victorian England must be judged dull and brutish. Despite its exotic fantasies and romantic prose, despite its flowery euphemisms for the genitalia and for intercourse, Victorian erotica was reductive. At bottom, its writers saw sexual activity as a "natural," if secret, function—which may be why the erotic novels of the period seem so anti-human; to be fully human in all the meanings of the word is to be *un*natural. Intelligence and imagination civilize every area of the natural world, including the sexual.

What makes our lovemaking different from that of beasts is that we think about it; for human beings, the most important sexual organ is above the neck, rather than below the waist. One of the accomplishments of erotic literature is the literary transformation of an act which is innately mechanical into meaningful individual experience. By encrusting sexuality with symbolic meaning, erotic literature helps reclaim it for civilization.

The writers of Victorian erotica were unable to achieve this transformation because of cultural limitations. Significantly, there has not been an erotic literature in England since the close of the nineteenth century. If it had not been for certain French writers who took up the challenge of transformation in the first decades of the twentieth century, there would be no modern erotic literature.

In France, the decade from 1925 to 1935 was a period of intense activity in erotic literature; for a time, the field held the attention of writers as notable as André Malraux, Georges Bataille, Louis Aragon, Jean Cocteau, Maurice Sachs, Robert Desnos, Pascal Pia, Benjamin Peret, and Louis Perceau. Of course they had a tradition to draw upon: in that decade Baudelaire's *The Flowers of Evil* was being published, with the banned poems, in its entirety for the first time; and Sade, Apollinaire, Theophile Gautier and Pierre Louÿs were available in beautifully bound and illustrated limited editions. Even Alfred de Musset, a poet who achieved a forgettable respectability as one of the leaders of the Romantic Movement in nineteenth-century France, is credited with writing an erotic novel entitled *Gamiani*. It was the most popular erotic novel in the French language up until 1930, by which time it had gone through forty-one editions. *Gamiani* is a romantic novel about lesbianism, in which the author—like John Cleland—attempted to describe erotic activity without using obscenities.

A later romantic writer, Pierre Louÿs, wrote erotic

novels which are somewhat more interesting eight decades later. Louÿs is best known for a novel set in pre-Christian Alexandria called *Aphrodite*. *Aphrodite* would be classified as "soft-core" these days because it achieves its highly erotic atmosphere by suggestion rather than by statement. An explicitly erotic novel, *Mother's Three Daughters,* has also been attributed to him. Whether he wrote the second novel or not a comparison of the two will be useful because between them we can see illustrated the kind of erotic writing that appeared in France up until 1925. Louÿs is the most important French erotic novelist up to that point.

Aphrodite is the story of Chrysis, a spoiled, much sought after Alexandrian courtesan who makes the mistake of falling in love with the sculptor Demetrios. Chrysis asks Demetrios to prove his love for her by committing three crimes, and then discovers too late that it is she who will be punished for his crimes. Louÿs successfully recreates the pagan ambience of ancient Alexandria, particularly in his descriptions of the Temple of Aphrodite, where women from all over the world spent their lives as temple prostitutes. Louÿs' lush prose avoids the worst excesses of romanticism while presenting the case for the Dionysian approach to life simply and evocatively. He explains his view of the pagan attitude about sex in an author's preface.

> Love, with all its consequences, was, for the ancient Greek, the sentiment most virtuous and most fecund in grandeurs. They did not attach to it those ideas of shamelessness and immodesty which Israelite tradition, along with the Christian doctrine, has handed down to us. . . .
>
> As for me, I have written this book with the simplicity an Athenian would have brought to a relation of the same adventures. . . .

Aphrodite fits into the French Romantic tradition of literature rather easily; its antecedents may be found in the work of Gautier, Baudelaire, and Flaubert. *Mother's*

Three Daughters, on the other hand, fits only into the line of erotic literature. *Aphrodite* seems chaste in its sensuous evocations of the ancient world when placed next to the detailed descriptions of sexual activity found in *Mother's Three Daughters.* That novel contains some of the most powerfully obsessive characterizations of prostitutes ever realized in the genre. The protagonist is an unnamed young man of twenty who moves into a boarding house and finds that his next-door neighbors are a mother and three young daughters who are sexually insatiable. The action of the novel consists of chapter by chapter accounts of the young man's sexual encounters with the four women. What is memorable about *Mother's Three Daughters* is the appetite for sexual variety the author ascribes to the female characters— a voracity which is made more powerful by his skill with dialogue and characterization.

These different approaches to erotic writing, one soft, evocative, and within a conventional literary tradition, the other harsh, explicit and obsessive, represent between their extremes the kind of erotic novel that was being published in Europe between the late nineteenth century and 1925.

In this period there is only one other author of erotic novels whose work must be mentioned: the poet Guillaume Apollinaire. Apollinaire's status as a major figure in French poetry is secure. Although he died in 1918 of injuries suffered earlier in the First World War, it was he who first used the word *surrealist* (a literary method by which the automatic, uncensored responses of the unconscious are employed to create a dream world and transform ordinary reality) and his influence on later writers has been considerable. Yet this poet of delicate lyrics and *avant-garde* formulations had another career: he wrote two erotic novels, one so brutal it is pseudo-Sadean, *The Debauched Hospodar;* the other, *Memoirs of a Young Rakehell,* bucolic and almost certainly autobiographical. In addition, he was something of a scholar in erotic literature. He wrote prefaces to erotic books, assisted in their publication, and compiled bibliographies in the genre, a French Pisanus Fraxi.

The sadism of *The Debauched Hospodar* is casually excessive, so quick and gruesomely comic it is a parody of Sadean fiction rather than a sadistic novel. Mony Vibescu is a Roumanian "Hospodar" (equivalent to the title of sub-prefect in France) who becomes bored with the pleasures of Bucharest and decides that he must have a woman of Paris. He goes to say goodbye to a friend and finds him with two pretty girls. An orgy follows, in which Mony is buggered at pistol point by his friend. The pace is frenzied from the start, increasing in tempo as Mony arrives in Paris and immediately becomes involved with two women who urge him to beat them with a coachman's whip. As an indication of the degree of sadism in the novel, this flagellation scene comes to seem mild when compared with the range of debauchery Apollinaire employs: murders, necrophilia, cannibalism, impalements, the rape of a child by her father, even a black mass. Apollinaire deliberately set out to violate every moral convention, in order perhaps to demonstrate—by exaggeration to the point of mania—that nothing is out of bounds in literature. Unfortunately, although this demonstration succeeds as a *tour de force,* the novel suffers from a lack of characterization and a haphazard plot.

Memoirs of a Young Rakehell, the brief narrative of a boy's sexual awakening, is as different from *The Debauched Hospodar* as black is from white. As the boy learns about sex from spying on his sister and timidly attempting to seduce the family maid, an atmosphere of highly charged adolescent sexuality is slowly developed. Although obscenities are used freely, there is something sweetly innocent about the novelist's use of fanciful imagery in describing sexual acts.

> I grabbed the lovely, prettily dressed peasant girl's sturdy buttocks and as I fondled her breasts, planted a pair of savoury kisses full on her mouth.

She took it in the right spirit, but when I reached her love lips she said, blushing: "It's my period." Just my luck! I was as erect as a bare-footed friar, and she was looking at my prick good-naturedly. She played with it prettily. At least I could amuse myself with her hanging gardens. I opened her jacket and her breasts slipped into my waiting hands. Like the girl herself, they were freckled, but aside from that I saw nothing to reproach them for.

Memoirs of a Young Rakehell is as conventional an erotic novel as *The Debauched Hospodar* is unconventional; like Louÿs, Apollinaire was capable of both extremes.

Having described and compared, in the cases of both poets, different approaches to erotic writing by the same author, it seems appropriate to attempt to draw some tentative conclusions about these differences. Obviously, *Mother's Three Daughters* and *The Debauched Hospodar* fit into one category, and *Aphrodite* and *Memoirs of a Young Rakehell* into another. The first is assaultive, in that books like *The Debauched Hospodar* attempt to overwhelm the reader's sense by a shock treatment that is apt to horrify or repulse; this is the Dionysian impulse to destruction which found its literary expression in Sade. The second is seductive. Novels like *Aphrodite,* and *Memoirs of a Young Rakehell* to a lesser extent, attempt through a softer, more sensuous approach to seduce the reader into not only accepting the author's depiction of sexuality as an accurate reflection of the reader's own sexuality, but to entertain and stimulate as well. These two lines of erotic writing, the assaultive and the seductive, can be followed throughout the history of modern erotic literature. Between them, they enclose a majority of work in the genre, although there is a third mode, the philosophical, exemplified by the work of Georges Bataille.

Apollinaire's career as an erotic writer is the link between Sade in the eighteenth century, and the group of writers attracted to erotic literature in the late nineteen-twenties. Perhaps the most notable of these was a literary figure (speculation names Louis Aragon, the surrealist poet) who wrote a short, brilliant erotic novel entitled *Le Con d'Irène* under the pseudonym Albert de Routisie. (Literally translated, the title is *Irene's Cunt;* but it is *Irene* in the American edition, and in this chapter I have chosen to use English titles when possible.) *Irene* appeared in 1928, and as the French publisher Jean-Jacques Pauvert informs us in his preface to a recent American edition, 1928 was the year in which Jean Cocteau published his *White Paper,* and Georges Bataille published *Story of the Eye.*

"Eroticism must be made a value," André Malraux wrote in a preface to *Lady Chatterley's Lover* in 1932. The novelist *(Man's Fate)* and future Minister of Culture under Charles de Gaulle was also the secret publisher of an illustrated edition of Sade's *Juliette.* Like other writers of the period, Malraux sensed the importance of literary investigations into the erotic life, but he preferred to keep his contributions anonymous. For such reasons the definitive history of the period remains to be written.

We shall limit ourselves in this chapter to a few representative books, like *Irene.* Any examination of that remarkable work must begin with a brief consideration of surrealism as it touched upon eroticism. Primarily, surrealism had a liberating influence on literature. It admitted the uncensored unconscious, dream states, and free association into not only the creative process, but onto the printed page. Recognizing the liberating power of eroticism, the surrealists welcomed it with manifestos about amorous techniques while they defended exhibitionism, and began the movement to rehabilitate Sade. The intense activity of the surrealists in regard to literary eroticism provided a framework for the writers of the period, and produced at least two masterpieces: *Irene* and *The Story of the Eye.*

Irene is perhaps the first book we've considered other than Greek or Roman classics in which literary values are as important as erotic values. There is no question but that the novel derives its power from the eroticism which suffuses every page, but neither is there any question that it is a work of considerable literary merit. Many critics would argue that it transcends the genre, but that attitude avoids an important issue. It will arise again and again as we look at the history of modern erotic literature, so we had best deal with it now.

It seems to me that the genre must be seen as a pyramid in terms of categorizing the works within it. The broad base of our imaginary pyramid is that mass of formula fiction which fails to utilize the conventions of the genre in fresh or original ways. Above that is a smaller mass of novels which, although written to formula, are examples of writers working to the limit of their abilities. Novels like *Mother's Three Daughters* belong here. The next level is, of course, much smaller. It is composed of novels like *The Story of the Eye, Story of O,* and *Irene:* novels which, although based in eroticism, ignore the formulas of the genre and transcend its limitations. This highest level of the pyramid is often claimed for general literature, but it shouldn't be. Works like *Irene* demonstrate not only the superior ability of the novelist, but the fertility of the genre he chooses to work in. It is a ground rich in possibilities—both of theme and execution. The author of *Irene* chose this particular genre because it stimulated his own interests, because he had emotions and ideas which he could not express in another form.

Irene and other novels of its rank demonstrate the possibilities of the genre more than they transcend it. There is an ecology in literature which demands that books be judged in the context of the tradition in which they were written, not ripped away from it and criticized as if they were *sui generis.*

Let us see just how important eroticism is in the novel Albert Camus called ". . . the finest of all works touching on eroticism." Let us see if it would retain its power if castrated.

Irene begins and ends with vituperation of the bourgeois world. The opening pages threaten:

"Don't wake me up, for God's sake, you bastards, don't wake me up, look out I bite, I see red."

The stream of consciousness invective which follows is typically surrealist; the author owes a debt to Lautreamont's *Maldoror* (1868), a classic pre-surrealist text. Yet although the author declares, "Arranging everything into a story is a bourgeois mania," he follows his opening tirade with a reasonably realistic narrative. The narrator has journeyed to a small, dreary town in eastern France to stay with relatives until he receives enough money to live on his own. While he waits he dreams, takes long walks, and—in a state of constant sexual arousal—visits the town brothel. After having sex with one of the whores, she invites him to peek into the next room, where another whore is taking on three men at one time. The narrator is asked if the sight doesn't stimulate him, but his reflections reveal—as is true of the protagonists of so many erotic novels—the ambiguous nature of his erotic feelings. He had entered the bordello in a state of painful arousal, but once satisfied he perceives only awkward sadness in sexual relations.

> What sadness there is in all erotic performances! I think of the awkwardness of dogs in the street, flocking together and all trying to outfuck each other. The dogs in the next room wore boots, that was all.

Later, he adds, "The erotic idea is the worst mirror. The glimpses of oneself that one catches in it are enough to make one shudder." In his boredom the narrator is driven to compose a story, which he writes as he sits in cheap cafés. It is the story of a paralyzed old man sitting in a farmhouse who takes immense erotic pleasure in watching his daughter and other people make love in front of him. Over this story is set the figure of the half-real, half-phantom Irene, to whom the author pays homage with his erotic daydreams; but voyeurism is the chief erotic focus of the novel. The narrator spies on other customers in the brothel, feels revulsion at the sight, and then is moved because of boredom to write a story about another voyeur.

> Preserved from all the puerile concerns of men, I devote all my time here to sensuality. My reduced senses have attained extreme refinement, and I have come to know pleasure in its purity. . . . What true freedom in my apparent slavery. In the days when I had the power to walk and speak, I had to take account of others. I didn't dare to think, everything seemed criminal to me. I limited myself. . . .

Once again the Sadean theme of selfishness as the source of true sensuality is announced. Throughout the novel there is a concentration on eroticism which is absolute. Without it, Irene would be no more remarkable than another surrealist novel of the period, André Breton's *Nadja;* with it, *Irene* not only becomes one of the masterworks of erotic literature, but perhaps the finest novel produced by the surrealist movement.

The Story of the Eye by Georges Bataille appeared the year that *Irene* was published. Like *Irene,* it employs surrealist techniques to express sexual themes, but its eroticism is of a different order: direct, obsessive, and perverse. *The Story of the Eye* is a strange, fascinating novel which we will examine at length, but unlike *Irene* it is not an isolated, unsigned work from an author who made his career writing books on other themes. *The Story of the Eye* is one of a handful of erotic novels written by Bataille, who spent his life exploring the most provocative themes of eroticism.

Since Bataille is the most important and original mind to have written about eroticism in the twentieth century, a brief account of his career must preface an examination of his work and ideas.

Although his studies prepared Bataille for the historian's

role, his interests lay with philosophy and religion in his formative years. Later, he wrote about everything from art to sociology, from linguistics to ethnology. In the early nineteen-thirties he published several erotic novels, some of which remain untranslated. *The Story of the Eye, Madame Edwarda (The Naked Beast at Heaven's Gate), L'Anus Solaire, The Little One* are the works of a surrealistic imagination, despite their author's attacks on the movement. His major work, *Death and Sensuality, (L'Erotisme)* appeared in 1947 in France and fifteen years later in America. He died in 1962, and the importance of his ideas is still unrecognized in America.

Bataille's lack of recognition may be the result of a prose style that does not attempt to charm the reader, but to persuade him or her of the importance of the thought expressed. His assumptions are severe: that the reader accept eroticism as one of the two major themes of life, the other being death. His intelligence is of such breadth that no one could accuse him of being limited or partisan in his exploration of the apparently opposed themes of death and eroticism. His conviction that sexuality is the secret heart of life, as he writes in a preface to *Madame Edwarda.*

> I am by no means predisposed to think that voluptuous pleasure is the essential thing in this world. Man is more than a creature limited to his genitals. But they, those unavowable parts of him, teach him his secret.

What secret? Ecstasy? Death? "We do not attain ecstasy save when before the however remote prospect of death, of what destroys us." Although Bataille returns again and again to the idea of unity, he established no formal philosophy. That he is a philosopher is undeniable. He is the master of the philosophical mode of modern erotic literature. It is always interesting to see ideas elaborated upon in another form, to watch the philosopher become the novelist and to see how he breathes life into his thoughts. In Bataille's erotic novels the sexuality expresses his ideas so concretely that we are seldom distracted from real flesh, real sounds and smells, the way we are in most novels in which the characters strike us as visiting lecturers.

In *The Story of the Eye* we find a tone that is almost assaultive in its sexuality. Yet there is a formality about it, a cold intellectual hardness which puts a distance between the characters and the reader. It begins on an anguished note.

> I had a solitary upbringing; as far back as I am able to remember sexual things worried me. I was nearly sixteen when, upon the beach at X. . . , I met Simone, a girl of my own age.

He divines that Simone might share his anguish, and opens their relationship by sitting in a saucer of milk left for the cat, challenging her to do the same.

> Simone put the saucer on a little bench, adjusted herself, in front of me, her gaze steadily upon me; sat down, soaked her behind in the milk. For some time I remained motionless, the blood rising to my head, and trembling, while she watched my prick strain against my trousers.

This is one of the most charming introductions in erotic literature, both to the characters and to the tone of *The Story of the Eye.* The narrator retains his detached voice throughout, while what happens gets curiouser and curiouser. In the second chapter we see Simone breaking eggs by squeezing them in her buttocks. Eggs become a recurring motif through the book, an obsession with the characters, who have a few picaresque adventures and torment a poor girl named Marcelle as often as they can. They are shameless with each other, and the surrealistic absurdity of their fascination with eggs perfectly expresses Bataille's simultaneous exploration of eroticism. As in *Irene,* the characters are isolated and acidulous in their view of the rest of humanity. Nothing matters but their own pleasures:

Other men, other women had ceased to be of any interest to us. We dwelt upon Marcelle only, whose voluntary hanging, or clandestine burial, or funereal apparition we childishly imagined.

That isolation is at the core of so many erotic novels may be attributed to the fact that erotic writers are in one sense or another always writing down their own masturbation fantasies. This is an element which is seldom mentioned when discussing these writers, but it is an obvious consideration. Erotic literature is singular in the respect that it alone of all literary genres can stimulate not only emotional reactions, but a physical release. Depending upon the writer's ability, he will either transform his private fantasies into public fiction, or simply transcribe the raw fantasy, leaving the reader with nothing more interesting than a psychosexual case history. All of the writers discussed in this chapter have attempted the difficult, necessary task of making their private fantasies accessible to the public through artifice.

In Bataille's fiction isolation is the natural order of things, but unity—between mind and body, death and sensuality—is the goal toward which his characters move. The search for God, or even the struggle to define him, becomes a path to that goal.

As Bataille says in *The Little One*, the two most common human images are the cross and the penis. They are certainly the predominant images in his fiction. To Bataille God is an idea which provides a context for the discussion of evil, a much more complex category. Without a Christian God evil would not exist, and evil—suffering, guilt, sensuality—is necessary for the transformation of experience. *The Little One* is a brief introduction to Bataille's notions of God and evil and how they are linked. "Indirectly, the consciousness of an impossible, dwelling in the depths of things, unites men. . . ."

The "impossible" is one of the definitions of God in

Bataille's thought; unification with the "impossible" is loss of self.

> I throw myself at the impossible head-on: given over to others—intimately united—writing bare-bellied. Like a repulsed woman, eyes empty, without personal existence.

Evil is a means of attaining unity, of achieving the most intense level of existence.

> How can this be evil if in the end it is man's good? This evil rejects calm, sets aside the guarantee of happiness: it sacrifices life, consumes it dangerously, pledges it to the sacred, to anguish.

In *Madame Edwarda*, the title character is a whore; she is also the embodiment of God. Without irony, Bataille writes of her in religious and erotic terms which, far from being contradictory, only serve to heighten the spiritual experience which is the climax of *Madame Edwarda*. Bataille's thought is essentially religious, despite his unorthodox definitions of God; the most enlightening of these definitions is found in *The Little One*. "God is worse or more distant than evil, is the innocence of evil."

The characters in Bataille's fiction are innocents in this context, struggling in their isolation toward unity, using "evil" as the means toward reunion with God. The nature of their innocence is revealed by the revulsion they often feel about sexuality. In *Madame Edwarda* the narrator reacts with loathing to the sight of the whore's vagina—which she calls "the old rag and ruin."

All the themes of Bataille's fiction are elaborated upon in his most important book, *Death and Sensuality*, which is subtitled "a study of eroticism and the taboo." It is a difficult and brilliant book, this summation of the thinking of a lifetime, and in its first few pages Bataille draws attention to the importance of the religious experience to eroticism.

> I believe that eroticism has a significance for mankind

that the scientific attitude cannot reach. Eroticism cannot be discussed unless man too is discussed in the process. In particular, it cannot be discussed independently of the history of religions. . . .

Let me stress that in this work flights of Christian religious experience and bursts of erotic impulses are seen to be part and parcel of the same movement.

This emphasis on religion is made even before Bataille defines eroticism.

Eroticism, unlike simple sexual activity, is a psychological quest independent of the natural goal: reproduction and the desire for children. From this elementary definition let us now return to the formula I proposed in the first place: eroticism is assenting to life even in death.

Death is another way of attaining unity, and has as important a place in Bataille's thought as religion. Death breaks down our individual, disconnected beings and brings us into harmony with the order of things, which is continuous and unbroken. It performs the same function, in this regard, as eroticism.

And then, beyond the intoxication of youth, we achieve the power to look death in the face and to perceive in death the pathway into unknowable and incomprehensible continuity—that path is the secret of eroticism and eroticism alone can reveal it. . . .

What I have been saying enables us to grasp in those words the unity of the domain of eroticism open to us through a conscious refusal to limit ourselves within our individual personalities. Eroticism opens the way to death. Death opens the way to the denial of our individual lives.

Evil—which in *Death and Sensuality* is allied with the Freudian idea of taboo—is necessary to existence in Bataille's formulation because it makes us feel the anguish of mind which is the experience of sin. That terror found at the heart of sensuality helps us escape our individual, discontinuous beings and become one with the continuity of existence.

The essays in *Death and Sensuality* are divided into two sections: Taboos and Transgressions, and Aspects of Eroticism. In the first part Bataille discusses eroticism in inner experience, the link between taboos and death, transgression, murder, hunting and war, marriage and the orgy, prostitution and Christianity. The common thread running through all these topics is the importance of taboo—of a sense of evil—as the motivating impulse pushing us toward unity with existence, which is ultimately achieved in death. In the second part, Bataille deals with the work of Alfred Kinsey and Sade, and incest, mysticism and sensuality, sanctity and solitude. These subjects are vehicles for Bataille's ideas about the relationship of sensuality to death.

Before concluding our review of Bataille's work, let us summarize his themes; they will recur again and again in the history of modern erotic literature. His fictional characters exist within "the innocence of evil." They are isolated not only from other people, but from conventional feeling; their transgressions are committed to achieve that sensual disorder which is the prelude to death. The relationship between sensuality and death is religious, for, although they are superficially opposed to each other, they are the only means we possess of approaching unity with existence.

Bataille has dedicated *Death and Sensuality* to Michel Leiris, and acknowledges his influences in the foreword to that book.

> . . . my own endeavours have been preceded by *Le Miroir de la Tauromachie* by Michel Leiris, in which eroticism is envisaged as an experience wedded to life itself; not as an object of scientific study, but more deeply, as an object of passion and poetic contemplation.

At this date the only book of Leiris' available in English translation is *Manhood* (1963). *Manhood* is a meditation on the author's life between the two world wars in which surrealism and classical mythology are employed to reveal and pursue certain sexual and psychological truths about himself.

From Bataille's speculations about the nature of eroticism we turn to the French novelists Genet, Klossowski, Réage and Arsan, from intellectual abstraction back to the fictional narrative that explores eroticism by poetic rather than intellectual means. First, however, it will be necessary to refer to some comments made by Jean-Paul Sartre on the work of one of these novelists, Jean Genet.

They are from Sartre's lengthy study of Genet, *Saint Genet, Comedian and Martyr* (1952). Sartre tells us that Genet's novels, particularly the first, *Our Lady of the Flowers* (1943) were not written in order to communicate, but so the author could masturbate over the images of his own fantasies. *Our Lady of the Flowers* was written in a prison cell that imposed upon the young erotic artist the isolation most novelists are free to choose for themselves. In his isolation, Genet fantasizes about past lovers with bright, allegorical names like Divine, Darling, Mimosa, and Seck Gorgui, and imagines himself making love with them. His sometimes gaudy rhetoric is a means to the end of sexual release. He begins as a brilliant transcriber of private fantasies, with no thought of making them accessible to the public. Sartre writes:

> Thus far, there is no art. Writing is an erotic device. The imaginary gaze of the gentle reader has no function other than to give the word a new and strange consistency. The reader is not an end; he is a means, an instrument that doubles the pleasure, in short a voyeur despite himself.

Yet—having written and published *Our Lady of the Flowers*—Genet becomes an artist, primarily because he manages to convince us that his inverted view of the world is as valid as the moral system that has rejected him.

> The world has isolated him as if he were pestiferous, it has cooped him in. Very well, he will intensify the quarantine. He will sink to depths where no one will be able to

reach him or understand him; amidst the turmoil of Europe, he will enjoy a ghastly tranquility. He rejects reality and, in order to be even more certain that he will not be recaptured, logic itself. . . . In short, we are confronted with a regression toward infantilism, toward the childish narcissism of the onanist.

One is bored in a cell; boredom makes for amorousness. Genet masturbates. . . . No wonder *Our Lady* horrifies people: it is the epic of masturbation.

Sartre's understanding of the basic impulse beneath Genet's novel writing reemphasizes our earlier conclusions about the stages of erotic art, from masturbatory fantasy to public fiction. His perceptions about Genet's work are so acute one regrets that he himself has not written erotic fiction. Sartre says that Genet's novels begin as masturbatory fantasies but become something greater because of Genet's rejection of the conventional moral order. For it, the artist substitutes an upside-down world in which every despised attribute, every crime—cowardice, homosexuality, betrayal, theft, murder—is upheld as a positive value. He holds a mirror up to the moral codes of the world, and they are reflected back in mirror writing.

Genet's five novels tend to blur in the reader's mind into one huge work on the same themes. Certainly the same type of character inhabits each book. In different guises, with resplendent names, they are nevertheless all variations on either the criminal or homosexual personality, transformed into radiant heroes by the gorgeous language Genet uses to describe them, language Sartre calls "stolen, faked, poeticized." But it is precisely Genet's gift of language which makes him an artist.

His literary method is at the service of his vision: the conventional world has rejected him—his criminality and his homosexuality—and he rejects it in turn by composing narratives which defy literary convention in their lack of traditional narrative form. Genet substitutes the logic of dreams for the standard logic of plotting; instead of a movement forward, we experience in his prose a drifting movement—that of the dreamer who switches from dream to dream as images, usually erotic, catch his fancy.

Unlike Bataille, unlike Sartre, Genet is not a philosopher. Instead he is perhaps the purest artist in French erotic writing. He has a stance toward the world: that his created universe, the reverse of ours in its values, is nevertheless as valid as ours, as "real." He persuades us of its reality by the power of his language, which is pure because it has no point to make. It simply heightens those moments of eroticism for which Genet exists. Its purpose is to give pleasure to the writer, and if it succeeds in communicating pleasurable feelings to the reader that is secondary to Genet's intentions. *Our Lady of the Flowers, Miracle of the Rose, Funeral Rites, Querelle of Brest,* and *The Thief's Journal* are chapters in one long autobiographical fantasy spun out of sequence by the dreamer Genet.

Now let us look at Genet as an erotic writer, which he is before anything else. Genet's approach to eroticism is seductive rather than assaultive. Occasionally he uses an obscenity, but it is always in a romantic context, as in the last page of *Our Lady of the Flowers* when he asks that his lover, Darling, be portrayed by a dotted line drawn around his prick. Yet make no mistake: every line of Genet's arises from an erotic impulse—even when he describes a crime he has commited.

> All by itself the murderer's hand seeks his penis, which is erect. He strokes it through the sheet, gently at first, with the lightness of a fluttering bird, then grips it, squeezes it hard; finally he discharges into the toothless mouth of the strangled old man. He falls asleep.

Despite the horror of the act, this passage is almost chaste in its description of sexuality. Genet avoids the brutal possibilities inherent within the description in order to preserve his trance-like portrayal of the murderer as saint and hero. The reader may be repulsed, but not in the way he might be by the same scene in *The Debauched Hospodar*. He will continue to read, seduced by Genet's ability with language, and by the dream state the language evokes.

Genet's eroticism is indirect but pervasive. Every physical description includes a reference to a character's genitals, for instance; and every character's actions are described in terms appropriate only to a lover writing about them. Genet has the ability to overpower the reader with his own physicality. His images are invariably sensuous: "No other book brings us in such close physical contact with an author," Sartre writes. We taste, smell, and feel the way Genet wants us to.

Bataille's theme, "the innocence of evil" is applicable to Genet's attitude toward God, but God to Genet is more political than metaphysical, although in the end these two words are synonymous. God represents the established order of things to Genet; without God, his universe would become invalid. Thus the concept of God is necessary, as is the concept of sin.

This, of course, is true for a majority of erotic writers. To the conventional world, sexuality is transgression, and transgression is the erotic writer's means of entrance into our psyches. Transgression is a powerful instrument in the hands of a writer like Genet or Bataille, but for it to have its effect there must be a God—or a social order—to rebel against.

Genet's contribution to erotic literature is that he uses transgression not to shock, as most erotic writers do, but to convince us of the validity of the universe he has created. For him, transgression is the norm, and his characters—transgressors against criminal or sexual codes—are heroes of the most exalted kind.

All of the erotic writers we have been discussing write within a moral context. Their themes depend upon the con-

cepts of good and evil, of God and the devil. They may over-
turn or reverse the conventional definitions of these abstrac-
tions, but the worlds they create require a moral framework.
This is no less true of a novel like *Story of O* (1954), about
which the critic Jean Paulhan has written, "if there is one
word which comes to mind when I think of *O*, that word is
decency."

The *Story of O* was published under a pseudonym,
Pauline Réage. Some of the notoriety this novel has attracted
may be attributed to speculation over the identity of the
author. For critical purposes ascertaining the name of the
author is not important; knowing the author's sex is, however. Names like André Malraux, Henri de Montherlant, Ray-
mond Queneau, André Pieyre de Mandiargues have been
suggested in the past, but at this point the most likely candidate for authorship appears to be the literary critic Domi-
nique Aury. The sex of the author is important because O,
the protagonist, is a woman who becomes the slave of a group
of men who use her the way they would use an ash tray. If a
man wrote *Story of O* it would remain a masterpiece of
erotic fiction, but it would lose much of its persuasive dialecti-
cal power; female authorship gives the theme of the book
an added political dimension.

Story of O is, on the surface, neo-Sadean. The author
has limited herself to the formulas of sado-masochistic novels
in her use of whips, chains, rings, leather, and branding irons
—all the paraphernalia of pornographic hackwork. Yet from
these melodramatic trappings of sexuality she has fashioned
a book of cruel elegance and intelligence.

O is a fashion model who goes for a ride with her boy-
friend one day. In the taxi he has her remove her underwear,
and then he delivers her to a house into which she is introduced as a sexual slave. The rest of the novel is the narrative
of her time in captivity, during which she is totally degraded.
Yet she accepts her role with a willingness born of great

strength—the strength of a woman who has chosen her course, and who has the ultimate power to say no at any time. This is the point of *Story of O:* the peculiar freedom that exists within slavery. Which of us does not remember the free existence we led as children, when we had nothing to worry about beyond our own preoccupations? The masters—our parents—had the responsibility of feeding and clothing us, and of making most of our decisions for us. Children enjoy a greater freedom than their parents simply because they don't have adult responsibilities. Perhaps it is for the same reason that men enlist in the military, or take jobs with paternalistic corporations.

Of course the theme of *Story of O* is more complex than this approach, but it suggests possibilities of interpretation which may aid the reader in understanding a book that is open to misinterpretation.

The actions of characters in erotic fiction are usually extreme. They push beyond acceptable, civilized limits in their transgression upon others or themselves. O moves in the course of the novel from a rather simple level of degradation to a much deeper and more profound level in which she totally surrenders her own being—even to the point of death.

Other critics have noted that the difference between *Story of O* and Sade's novels is that Sade's victims are unwilling captives, while O is a willing prisoner of love. In a sense her captors are her prisoners because they need her in order to realize their pleasures; she uses them for her own purposes, but she could leave them if she chose. The balance of power in *Story of O* is not what it seems.

Above all, *Story of O* is a novel about love, love pushed to its limits. This view of the novel is confirmed by the author in her introduction to the sequel to *Story of O, Return to the Chateau* (1969). In that introduction, entitled "A Girl In Love," and in her preface to another writer's pseudonymously published erotic novel, *The Image,* Réage explains her novels along the same lines. I have chosen

> A man in love . . . is the master, so it seems, but only if his lady friend permits it! The need to interchange the roles of slave and master for the sake of the relationship is never more clearly demonstrated than in the course of an affair. Never is the complicity between victim and executioner more essential. Even chained, down on her knees, begging for mercy, it is the woman, finally, who is in command.

These words are taken from the preface to *The Image.* The following is from *Return to the Chateau.*

> . . . Sade made me understand that we are all jailers, and all in prison, in that there is always someone within us whom we enchain, whom we imprison, whom we silence. By a curious kind of reverse shock, it can happen that prison itself can open the gates to freedom.

Return to the Chateau is a brief continuation of *Story of O,* another possible ending, in which O undergoes more of the tortures of love. It adds another variation to the theme of freedom in slavery, when O thinks to herself that the chains she wears are marks of pride because "they proclaimed that the person who had imposed them upon her loved her enough to set her thus apart from all others." Great love is required for anyone to take upon himself the responsibility for another person, and in Réage's fiction this responsibility is absolute.

The Image, published under the pseudonym Jean de Berg in 1956, is a simpler, briefer novel which addresses itself to the same themes as *Story of O.* A young man is attracted to a strange woman, Anne, who is the slave of an older woman named Claire. Claire demonstrates her absolute mastery of Anne to the young man, allows him to enjoy her slave, and then reverses roles, becoming the young man's slave. As the novel ends, he is having intercourse with her as she cries out that she loves him. In *The Image* and in Réage's two novels we find three of the most fully developed treatments of the theme of love as submission to the will of another in all of modern erotic literature. Its means of expression is a cruel eroticism which although explicitly detailed is saved by the purity of the authors' style from vulgarity.

Love and power also appear as themes in the work of Pierre Klossowski, a theologian and Sade scholar who wrote two difficult and strange novels, using the same characters in both: *Roberte ce Soir* (1953) and *The Revocation of the Edict of Nantes* (1959). Octave is an elderly ecclesiastic married to a serious but beautiful young wife, Roberte; their nephew Antoine completes the triangle. In *Roberte ce Soir* Klossowski has returned to the eighteenth-century philosophical dialogue in order for his characters to discuss the relationship between the body and the soul. As the body is the envelope of the soul, any sensual expression of the body is permissible because it may be a path to spiritual progress. *Roberte ce Soir* begins with a treatise written by Octave about the relationship between a host and his guest, in which he invites guests to make love to his wife using the most baroque reasoning ever found in an erotic novel. In *The Revocation of the Edict of Nantes*, using the diary form, Klossowski has Roberte explore the world of sexual perversion by retracing her past life.

Both Octave and Roberte use eroticism as a means to spiritual progress, and after the slightest sexual incident examine their reactions in microscopic intellectual and emotional detail. God is often invoked in both novels, but unlike the God of Bataille, this is an orthodox Catholic God. The tortured reasoning of the characters reflects Klossowski's theological studies with the Dominicans to such an extent that he may be regarded as the only erotic writer whose ideas are worked out within an acknowledged religious context.

A majority of the French erotic writers we have been discussing assume a direct relationship between religious concerns and eroticism. The last of them we shall comment on has taken this relationship one step further, to formulate a religion of sexuality. This is the author of *Emmanuelle* (1967) and *Emmanuelle II* (1968), "Emmanuelle Arsan" the pseudonym of Maryat Rollet-Andriane.

Emmanuelle is less cerebral than most of the novels discussed so far, and more sensuous in its descriptions; it does have ideas to advance—important ideas—but unfortunately they are delivered as lectures. The protagonist, Emmanuelle, is a young married French woman who comes to Bangkok to join her diplomat husband Jean. Her erotic adventures begin on the plane trip to Thailand, and continue in Bangkok, where she meets women at the country club who seem to talk and think of nothing else but sex. They ask her if she will join them in their erotic games, and although she is reluctant at first, she ultimately becomes one of them when a brash young girl visits her and they masturbate together while gazing at each other's bodies.

Emmanuelle quickly becomes infatuated with a tall American model, has her first homosexual experience, falls under the influence of an older man named Mario who becomes her sexual guru, and has numerous affairs, each more purely erotic than the last. Her husband instead of feeling possessive of her encourages her affairs, stating that he married her because she was sexually insatiable. Slowly, every person, detail, and object in *Emmanuelle* becomes eroticized until the novel resembles a hothouse full of exotic flowers.

Emmanuelle II (published in France as *Emmanuelle, The Anti-Virgin*) is a continuation of the narrative of Emmanuelle's erotic explorations. It is less of a novel than the first because it is more of a treatise than a story, but for that reason—that important ideas about the nature of eroticism are expressed—it is more interesting than its predecessor.

Emmanuelle possesses a purity of form and approach which
Emmanuelle II has discarded for the lengthy exposition of
ideas, principally through the character of Mario, the middle-
aged *eroteur* of the first novel. Once again Emmanuelle
pursues her love affairs, but this time it is Mario and his
exhortations to the young woman which give focus to the
book.

> The prime virtue I attribute to eroticism is simply this:
> it breaks down the wall of solitude. At long last, it gives hu-
> mans a taste for other humans. And I am convinced that it
> can succeed, and succeed far better than any other discipline.
> . . . To make love to more than one body in no way injures
> the idea of love, nor does it betray that idea: it is the gateway
> to an abundant life, in which love multiplies the lover and at
> the same time prevents him from amputating the beloved.

Rather floridly written (Mario is long-winded) but
nevertheless a persuasive argument against monogamy, one
of the bases of a repressive culture. The idea of the multipli-
cation of love through eros is more than a libertine's plea in
its almost painful idealism. Further, there is the idea that
eroticism multiples the possibilities of life.

> What I am saying is that those who are blind to eroticism
> are equally blind to all of life's other purposes. And those for
> whom the flesh is worthless find the values of the spirit
> equally incomprehensible.

There is only a semblance of plot to hold together the
set speeches and sexual description in *Emmanuelle II*, but
there is a forward movement in Emmanuelle's progress
toward total freedom, and her embodiment of the religion
of eros. Although Maryat Rollet-Andriane takes a different
approach to love—finding it in freedom rather than slavery—
than Pauline Réage, the two women writers share a perception of eroticism as the highest expression of spiritual love.
When one summarizes the contributions French writers
have made to modern erotic literature in the past half cen-

tury, it is evident that their approaches to form have been nearly as important to the genre as the ideas they have explored. Albert de Routisie and Georges Bataille demonstrated how the methods of surrealism might be applied to the erotic novel; Apollinaire reaffirmed the validity of the assaultive approach in *The Debauched Hospodar*, freeing erotic novelists from the euphemistic conventions of Victorian erotica, just as Pauline Réage reclaimed the Gothic form for modern erotic writing and Jean Genet brought to the genre the possibility of writing narrative based on the logic of fantasy rather than plot.

The protagonists of modern French erotic writing are isolated in their attitude toward the world, and see transgression through eroticism ("evil") as a means of surrendering their painful individuality. Their quest for unity with the world is usually religious, and has one of two ends: love or death.

IV

PUBLISHED IN PARIS

> For years, ever since the first stirs in my groin, I'd hungered, like my brothers, for forbidden works, forbidden images. Equivalent to an ancient quest, Hebraic word-mania. . . . It's fitting that the forbidden sacred words of my early quest were not those Kaballistic glyphs and maps but smudgy-covered worn paperbacks from Paris. . . . These books and words within their smirched fronts were capable of strong magic. . . .
>
> —DAVID MELTZER

THE IMPORTANCE OF certain publishers in the history of erotic literature cannot be overemphasized. Indeed, their tastes and their receptivity to new kinds of erotic writing have been almost as influential in the development of the genre as the authors they have published. In this century the most important publisher of erotic writing in English has been The Olympia Press, the successor to The Obelisk Press, which was started in Paris in the early nineteen-thirties.

The publisher of The Obelisk Press was an expatriate Englishman named Jack Kahane, and the first book to appear under the imprint of his new press was his own erotic novel, *Daffodil*. It was followed by a number of books which have become modern classics, including Henry Miller's *Tropic of Cancer*, published in 1934. Kahane also published—in the years between 1934 and his death in 1939—Lawrence Durrell's first novel, *The Black Book*, Frank Harris's erotic autobiography, *My Life and Loves*, and books by Cyril Connolly, Anaïs Nin, and James Joyce, as well as Miller's *Tropic of Capricorn* (1939).

Here was a publisher who was interested in something more than financial gain; the erotic fantasies he published supported the printing of literary works of little commercial promise. Kahane's son, Maurice Girodias (he took his mother's name) revived The Obelisk Press after the Second World War and operated it according to equally high standards.

In the spring of 1953, Girodias founded The Olympia Press, and in the next twelve years published in his plain green Traveller's Companion Series not only some of today's brightest literary names (Samuel Beckett, Vladimir Nabokov, Jean Genet, William Burroughs, and J. P. Donleavy among others) but dozens of serious erotic novels.

The writers of these novels—Harriet Daimler, Alexander Trocchi, Marcus Van Heller, Ataullah Mardaan, Terry Southern, Mason Hoffenberg, Akbar Del Piombo, Henry Jones, William Talsman, James Sherwood, and others—approached the writing of what Girodias fondly called "d.b.'s." (dirty books) with high spirits and genuine talent. The novels they wrote for Girodias comprise a new wave of erotic writing in English.

Most of these writers were American or English expatriates. They were young men and women with serious literary ambitions in the Paris of the fifties; Girodias paid them small advances and set them to work producing erotic novels for sale to English-speaking tourists. Exotic, often funny pseudonyms were dreamed up (Carmencita de las Lunas was one of the more inspired of these) and novels, which were often written in no more than a week, were printed in editions of five thousand copies each. When Girodias ran out of money he would write blurbs for non-existent books, and then, when the orders for these came in, assign writers to come up with novels to fit his fanciful descriptions of them. It isn't a method of publishing to be recommended if erotic novels of quality are to be produced, but it worked because Girodias was fortunate in his authors, and encouraging of their wildest efforts. His authors were gifted writers, and literary talent will surface in the most improbable circumstances.

Twenty years later at least a dozen of The Olympia Press novels published in the fifties still seem fresh and imaginative forays in the genre. Before we look at them, however, we should consider for a moment some of the work which influenced them.

A few of these novels are nostalgic parodies of Victorian erotica; a larger number make use of the French surrealist tradition discussed in the last chapter; many are Sadean in their implications; a humorous view of sexuality seems the most prevalent approach, however. Their books possess buoyance of spirit, a sense of fun and adventure in the midst of misery.

In this sense the literary godfather of these writers is Henry Miller. Miller's books need not be analyzed here. Although the erotic sections of his novels once caused a sensation, and although he was extremely important both to Olympia Press (Girodias published his later books as his father had published the early ones) and to the development of erotic writing, there has been ample comment on his work. It is sufficient to point out that Miller's tone, first of all—that optimistic, experience-embracing voice of the *Tropics*—and secondly, his freedom in describing his sexual adventures, were of great importance to the writers who published under The Olympia Press imprint.

The most notable of these writers is a Scotsman named Alexander Trocchi, who first published with Girodias under the pseudonym of Frances Lengel. His books—*Young Adam, White Thighs, Thongs, School for Wives, Helen and Desire,* and *The Carnal Days of Helen Seferis*—all appeared in the fifties when Trocchi was living in Paris and editing the literary magazine *Merlin*.

In 1967 Brandon House, a California publishing firm, reprinted five of Trocchi's erotic novels, some with new postscripts by the author. In his postscript to the Brandon House edition of *Helen and Desire,* Trocchi tells us that it was the first of the works he wrote under the Frances Lengel pseudonym, and that it was written in just over eight days in 1953. He seems most satisfied with the lightness of touch he was able to achieve in writing the novel, and certainly, it has its comic aspects; but *Helen and Desire* offers more than deft entertainment.

Trocchi's heroine is Helen Smith. She tells her story in a manuscript which has supposedly been "found" by a French policeman in Algeria, who got it from an Arab he'd picked up. At the beginning of the novel she tells us that she is a prisoner in an Arab tent, somewhere in the desert. After this brief introduction she relates her life story.

She grew up in an isolated village in Australia, and decided that she had to escape her narrow background. One day after she has been swimming naked in the sea and has masturbated herself against a tree trunk, she sees one of the local men attempting to rape a village girl. She sees in the man her chance to escape the village, and allows him to make love to her, suggesting that they run away to a large city. He offers to marry her, but Helen has other ideas. In one paragraph Trocchi shows us his ability not only to write from a woman's point of view (the novel is written in the first person) but to create an independent woman character. In *Helen and Desire,* and in all of Trocchi's erotic novels, strong women play leading roles, which in itself is unusual in erotic fiction by men. Helen's anger at the man's proposal indicates the level of sympathetic understanding with which Trocchi approaches his female characters.

> What a fool he was! The thought of marriage had never crossed my mind. To be a house slave as my mother had been, to lose my freedom and adapt myself to his absurd male requirements! That was my first experience of this kind of idiot male presumption—why do they assume that because we have need of their bodies we will be willing to submit ourselves to the drab pattern of their everyday existence? If a man is poor and must work, what an overbearing impertinence to expect a beautiful woman to harness herself to his venal and constricted existence! Such men should be housed in a stable after their toil and, if it is a woman's pleasure, they should be loaned to her for her occasional enjoyment. . . .

Once she is in a city Helen leaves the man and takes another train to Sydney, where her money is stolen and she goes to work for a pimp whose business is providing beautiful young women for his female clientele. When Helen tires of prostitution she uses another man to take her out of Australia, and her adventures continue in various eastern ports until she reaches North Africa, where a man betrays her and she ends up the prisoner of desert nomads.

It is an exotic, melodramatic narrative, always lively, and obviously written with great gusto. Trocchi's handling of eroticism is seductive and literate, although at times he lapses into purple prose in his sexual descriptions. Although the erotic episodes are frequent, the book is unremittingly sensual in its other physical descriptions as well. Helen is an utterly sexual being, one of the best descriptions of the type in erotic literature, and the perfect vehicle for Trocchi's principal theme, one we discussed in connection with Georges Bataille: the obliteration of the individual consciousness through eroticism.

These are Helen's reflections on the subject just after a scene in which her body has been used by one of her Arab captors:

> . . . Once again I have experienced the terrible joy of annihilation, the deliverance of my whole being to the mystery of sensual union, and this time with a male whom I would not recognize in daylight. . . .

But Helen retains her independence outside of sexual union:

> I rejoice again in my separateness, in the vital isolation that makes it possible for a human being to collide, to coalesce, and for a short while to coexist with another.

The Carnal Days of Helen Seferis is a sequel to *Helen and Desire* in which an English detective named Anthony Harvest is hired to find the missing Helen. Her manuscript is given to him and he goes to Algeria to find her. Trocchi calls *The Carnal Days* "light entertainment," an apt description of this double parody of both the erotic novel and Ian Fleming's James Bond character. Anthony Harvest does find Helen after a search in which adventure is as much an element as sex. *Carnal Days* is Trocchi's least important novel, but even in it we find unusual, interesting characters, and a plot as enjoyable as an adventure serial.

Trocchi wrote *Young Adam* in twelve days in 1952, and commented fifteen years later that he regarded it then as "something of an achievement." Although *Young Adam* may be loosely classified as an erotic novel because its central situation revolves around sex, it stands apart from Trocchi's other erotic novels because it is less formulistically written; it is also less successful. It is the story of a young man who works on a coal barge in Scotland with a married couple. He seduces the wife under the nose of her husband, and the scenes in which the wife's gradual sexual awakening is delineated are first rate; unfortunately the novel is burdened with a plot device older than Hollywood: the hero is responsible for the death of his previous girl friend, but an innocent man is indicted for the crime. This device provides narrative tension, but it distracts from the erotic element which is the most interesting aspect of the novel.

White Thighs is Trocchi's most successful novel in the genre after *Helen and Desire*. Its erotic theme is sadomasochism, a theme which is developed by the creation of a character, Saul, who is thoroughly evil (he is a murderer) and triumphant, from beginning to end. Saul is an English orphan sent as a boy to live in America with his rich uncle and maiden aunts. He falls in love with his governess—a Russian Jewish woman named Anna—who exerts a strong sexual influence over him—to such an extent that when his uncle threatens to have her sent back to Russia, Saul poisons him. After this incident Saul is sent to England for his education and Anna marries a local wastrel. After graduation Saul returns to take over his uncle's estate, determined to reclaim Anna. He murders her husband and goes to claim her, but she is unexpectedly angry; she loved the man because he mastered her. Saul, seeing that their old relationship—in which she dominated him sexually—is no longer valid, assumes the dominant position and finds her receptive. The balance is tipped; Saul, who had regarded himself as submissive, takes the dominant position with Anna for the first time, only to fall himself under the sway of his muscular female cook. Together, he and the cook set up a dungeon in the basement of the house and enlist the other servants in their sadomasochistic fantasy. When the cook becomes too presumptuous, Saul murders her and becomes engaged to a local girl who seems suspiciously normal—until the last page, when the author hints that Saul has found his match. The woman, Vivian, is a mystery.

> Each of the other women had been essentially insecure, hiding behind mere prettiness, coquetry, grim morals, and in that insecurity lay the key to their self-abasement. They had delivered themselves over entirely to the will of another, like subjects of a totalitarian state, women deprived of a real God, victims of their own fatal isolation. Conflict had died with responsibiilty. They were "free."
>
> But Vivian, what of her?
>
> Was she—a young woman in perfect health, an acknowledged beauty, with more money than she would ever know what to do with—was she afraid of the responsibility of being herself?
>
> Much as I should have liked to think so, I thought it highly unlikely. Not yet certainly. In ten years' time, perhaps, if she had not by that time accepted the painful reality of being an individual, if deceived, disappointed, and powerless even with her great wealth to attain inner peace, she contemplated with the insane courage of a disillusioned woman of thirty the possibility of "dying" to herself in subjecting herself utterly and irrevocably to another's will—as I knew well from my own experinece, there was an obscene attraction in this—perhaps then . . .

The responsibility of being oneself can be escaped for awhile in the self-obliteration of the sexual act, particularly in a sadomasochistic relationship. This is perhaps Trocchi's most fully developed statement of a theme which he explores in more detail but with less success in two other novels: *School for Wives* and *Thongs*. Perhaps by the time he wrote them he was limited by the requirements of his publisher. He asserts this in his 1967 postscript to *Helen and Desire*: "M. Girodias' strictures had not yet become, as they certainly did later, a tiresome limitation."

Despite these limitations, fifteen years later, Trocchi felt proud enough of his erotic *oeuvre* to put his own name on the novels reissued by Brandon House. And despite the fact that he stopped writing erotic fiction, and indeed, stopped publishing books altogether, with the exception of his excellent autobiography *Cain's Book* in 1960, he said in London in 1970, "Writers should be proud to take on the honored name of pornographer." In 1967 he had written, "In certain situations that modern writer lacks integrity who shies away from the obscene."

It may be that his publisher's strictures helped more than they hurt, because they were a challenge for him to overcome. In his best erotic novels he transforms the conventions of erotic literature to fashion highly entertaining, brilliantly written essays on some of the most important themes of the genre. The way he presents the theme of the loss of self through sexuality offers the average reader a more accessible path to understanding it than Bataille does; that he accomplishes this with tongue in cheek is to his credit.

Men like Trocchi who write erotic novels from a woman's point of view run the risk of seeming inauthentic, particularly when they portray the loss of self through sex. If a man writes a scene in which a woman enjoys being raped, female readers may well put the book aside with the argument that men don't know the horror of rape. But this argument is political in nature, and good writers transcend the limitations of gender loyalty in their creation of characters who act according to the dictates of emotion rather than politics.

The proof of this may be seen in the work of women like Pauline Réage and Harriet Daimler—both writers who have written novels in which female characters welcome, even demand sexual abuse. Iris Owens, under the pseudonym of Harriet Daimler, wrote a novel for The Olympia Press in the mid-fifties that Girodias titled *Darling*, the story of a woman artist living in Greenwich Village who is the victim of a violent rape and who becomes obsessed with finding her rapist—for revenge, but also in order to repeat the experience.

The character, Gloria, is portrayed by Daimler as a rather frigid bitch who is sexually awakened by her rapist. Throughout the rest of the novel she conducts her own search for the man, her emotions split between love and hate for him. When she finally does find him, he doesn't remember assaulting her, but willingly participates in a reenactment of the rape. During it, she kills him. Vengeance is Gloria's primary motivation, but beyond that is her feeling that "she was a vessel in which he had carelessly deposited his soul"— and killed hers in the process. In order to regain her own soul, she has to kill him; she has to destroy the stranger who had taken possession of her, the stranger who prompts her to sexual aggression throughout the novel. None of the men she encounters are sexually adequate for her because she demands of each one that he recreate the overwhelming brutality of the rapist in his lovemaking.

What was most frightening was the thought that he might never have existed, that she had created him out of an incredible lust and sickness inside herself. As long as he was not her creation, she could live, searching for him and trying to have, for the final time, the experience he had given her.

Daimler is skillful at drawing Gloria's essential ambivalence: on one hand she would do anything for the rapist if he would only return to her, but on the other hand she wants back the self he has stolen from her.

Some women, she knew, chose to live their subjugation. They discovered the chastised, tormented creatures they were and lived to feed their suffering. They looked for a master to punish them, to sate their craving for punishment. . . . Punished for what? For forgiveness, for a reprieve, for the sins of fathers and mothers and aunts and uncles and cousins. And finally for the sins of rage and appetite—the combined sins of all.

But Gloria, finally, does not choose to live her subjugation. She lives in the "closed world of self" in which she
feels no need for self-punishment.

In *Darling*, as in *Helen and Desire*, the theme of loss of
self is taken a step further. Like the characters in Trocchi's
fiction, the protagonists of these novels, while acknowledging
the importance of this sexual experience, nevertheless choose
to keep their individuality. Both characters accept the fact of
their essential isolation, but Helen seeks self-obliteration,
and Gloria is driven to near madness by it.

Daimler's sexual descriptions, unlike Trocchi's, are
brutally explicit; *Darling*, despite its melodramatic structure, is coldly realistic in its view of the world. Gloria has a
lover who is the opposite of the rapist: tender, sentimental,
and weak. Needless to say, she despises the man. Daimler's
portrayal of the bitch in *Darling* is superb, foreshadowing
her rendition of it in her first non-erotic novel under her
own name, *After Claude* (1972). She delineates the Greenwich Village milieu with an accuracy which is equally
deadly. Because of her distrust of sentimentality and romanticism, *Darling* stands at the other end of the spectrum from
most erotic novels written by women.

Only *The Woman Thing*, of the remainder of Daimler's
erotic novels, is comparable to *Darling* in seriousness of
theme and execution. It is the only one of her erotic novels
that is semi-autobiographical, and the only one besides
Darling which works on more than one level. Martha is a
young American expatriate living in Paris in a fleabag hotel
with an extravagant Scotsman named Macdonald. They talk
brilliantly and endlessly, fight violently, and make up in bed.
At times the dialogue is reminiscent of the magnificent
rhetoric Djuna Barnes put into the mouth of Dr. Mathew-
Mighty-Grain-Of-Salt O'Connor in *Nightwood* (1936).

Once again, *The Woman Thing* features a smart, aggressive woman who is ambivalent about being possessed by

a man. Daimler has made Martha less of a bitch than Gloria in *Darling*, and as the critic Seymour Krim said to Daimler, "It's one of the few books written by an American in which the man and woman actually *like* each other." In describing the couple, Daimler also talks about what she was trying to communicate in the book.

> A spontaneous and genuine sexual expression, of course, but beyond that, (the girl) is trying to find out how a man and woman might live and develop together. . . . I think the girl in my book is trying to get born. She is naive, as I was naive. She is available, aggressive, angry, good-natured and totally confused. I am sure that I was all these things. . . . The man in the book is a phantom man, unproductive, unconnected with the ambitious and goal-oriented world. He is, I guess, the male counterpart of what I was; the only type of man I could then imagine or tolerate. In Paris we played house, played marriage, played at being men and women, and, I hope, in the play, learned a few things.

Martha and Macdonald play house in bed, where they fight wittily—but warmly—over the little they have to eat, and how Martha's checks from home will be spent. There are enough erotic scenes so that the novel falls into the category of erotic literature, but the main focus of the book is the examination of a destructive relationship. Over and over Martha asks a sardonic Macdonald if they're together because they love each other or because of sex, and Martha's funny but desperate need to resolve the question provides the narrative thread. *The Woman Thing* is Daimler's most mature exploration of the ambivalence a woman feels who wants both to lose herself in love and somehow still retain her individuality.

Of all the writers who published with The Olympia Press in the fifties, an English civil servant who wrote under the name of Marcus van Heller was the most prolific. The first novel he wrote for Girodias was *Rape*, a book which seems perfectly representative of the eleven Olympia novels which followed it. Van Heller excels at the depiction of violence, and his characterizations of people like the rapist Harvey Crawford display a talent for writing in the assaultive mode of erotic fiction. In a postscript to the Brandon House reissue of *Rape,* van Heller comments on the frustration experienced by the rapist. Frustration and terror motivate the characters in his best work.

From the beginning van Heller exhibited a facility with narrative pacing that keeps the reader turning pages. Unfortunately, this very highly developed ability to tell a good story too often sacrifices character development to plot. His method is to anchor his narrative solidly in historical circumstances—ancient Rome and Egypt or Paris during the Algerian war (*Terror*) and to develop his themes from circumstances rather than the character.

Van Heller's range is wide, as befits a solidly professional novelist who always provides what the English call a "good read." His second novel, *The Loins of Amon,* is set in ancient Egypt; *Roman Orgy* is an erotic retelling of the Spartacus story; *The House of Borgia* follows Cesare and Lucrezia Borgia to their doom in fifteenth-century Italy; *Terror, The Wantons,* and *Nightmare* are contemporary novels of social content; *Cruel Lips* and *Kidnap* are thrillers; *Rape* and *Adam and Eve* are psychological novels. What is important is not that van Heller works in so many different areas of the novel, but that he does it so well. This list makes it apparent even in the work of a single author that the possibilities within the genre are unlimited.

Van Heller has written the familiar disclaimer that his primary motivation in doing them was satirical, that they were never seen other than as forms of "satire, humor. . . ."

. . . occasionally on a rainy afternoon we may have reminisced in the pages, or indulged our private fantasies. But on the whole the sexual passages were our least concern.

This plea doesn't hold water, even when it comes from the publisher himself, as when Girodias says in his anthology of Olympia Press writers of the fifties that they wrote parodies of the form. It obviously is untrue, as a glance at any of the novels discussed in this chapter will make clear.

Of course there are genuine satirists in the genre, and of The Olympia Press novelists of the fifties Akbar Del Piombo (the pseudonym of the painter Norman Rubington), Terry Southern, and Mason Hoffenberg are the most notable. Del Piombo's erotic satires began to appear in 1955. Among them are *The Double-Bellied Companion, Who Pushed Paula?, Skirts,* and *Cosimo's Wife or The Vengeance of a Duke.*

The hero of *Skirts,* Eddie Champdick, is an orphan with an unusual problem: he suffers from priapism. His unnatural limitless potency gets him into trouble when a Turk gets the idea that Eddie would be the perfect eunuch for middle eastern harems. Based on this premise, Eddie's adventures with spear in hand quickly move into the low comedy of absurdity. Del Piombo manages to combine humor with realistic descriptions of sex so that (unlike most satirical erotic novelists) his jokes don't deflate the sexual action.

This is also true of Mason Hoffenberg's approach to erotic satire. Hoffenberg, with Terry Southern, co-authored the most famous of erotic satires, *Candy,* under the pseudonym of Maxwell Kenton. Since *Candy* appeared in 1958 it has been reprinted several times, and made into a film. Because it is so well known I will refer to it only tangentially in discussing two less famous erotic comedies by Hoffenberg: *Until She Screams,* written under the rakish pseudonym of Faustino Perez, and *Sin for Breakfast* (1957) signed with the pseudonym Hamilton Drake.

Candy (1958) is a broadly written parody of the conventional genre novel in which a young girl is subjected to a sexual education (see *Fanny Hill* and *Justine*); but it also satirizes certain aspects of contemporary society, particularly the spiritual quest of the sixties. Candy is a naive young American girl whose search for a guru gets her into ridiculous situations in which she is constantly being taken advantage of. We may never know which of the authors was responsible for Candy's most outrageously exaggerated misadventures, but Terry Southern seems the best candidate because Mason Hoffenberg's approach in his other novels tends to be more subtle than the broad comedy of *Candy*.

The Faustino Perez pseudonym and the title *Until She Screams* indicate that Hoffenberg intended a takeoff on the standard Olympia Press d.b., the kind of hackwork we haven't discussed here; but the novel is a better entertainment and a better erotic novel than the d.b.'s it parodies so skillfully.

Until She Screams is set in Mexico. An ugly young Indian named Miguel is chopping wood when the lady who owns the estate where he works rides up and orders him to strip. Her sexual excitement humiliates him, and he decides to leave her estate when she humiliates him a second time by using him as a pawn in an erotic game. He turns up on the property of a poor Spaniard, Señor Lopez, who is afflicted with a nagging wife and a luscious but deranged stepdaughter named Lolita. Miguel and Señor Lopez become *bandidos,* and in the end Miguel has his revenge on the aristocratic woman who humilated him.

Hoffenberg's skillful rendering of the Mexican setting is an important factor in the construction of a narrative which may be read first as a good erotic novel and second as a gentle satire on the sexual foibles of his characters. His portrait of the lazy Spaniard Señor Lopez is the best characterization in a novel that succeeds in bringing to life a gallery of Mexican types.

The superiority of *Until She Screams* to the d.b.'s it is based on doesn't prepare us for the sophisticated self-consciousness of Hoffenberg's *Sin for Breakfast*, however. Here the title and the pseudonym are irrelevant to the content of the novel, which is constructed like one of those painted Russian dolls which opens up to reveal another, smaller doll inside, and one inside that, and so forth.

Trent is a wealthy American expatriate living in Paris with his beautiful but supposedly frigid wife Vivian. He spends his time failing to master the Chinese language and failing to achieve a satisfactory sexual relationship with his wife. One day he follows her to his friend Oliver's apartment and sees them making love. Instead of reacting like a jealous husband, he cultivates a relationship with Margot, Oliver's young girl friend. Margot writes d.b.'s for a Girodias-like publisher, and encourages Trent to write one by using her body to illustrate her points. Trent lusts after Margot with her teasing encouragement; she is willing to go so far as to display her genitals to him in the same room with Vivian and Oliver, and to lead him on at an uproarious Art Students' Ball. Trent begins a d.b., and writes a scene in which he rapes Margot, only to have Vivian discover his efforts. The novel ends when she proves to him that she too has been writing an erotic novel—*Sin for Breakfast*, by Hamilton Drake.

Sin for Breakfast is extraordinarily self-conscious, and one of the few novels that is directly about the genre itself. Hoffenberg gives us a wry self-portrait in the character of Trent, introduces "Faustino Perez" in the office of the Girodias character, and stimulates the speculation that Margot is Harriet Daimler. In the context of an enjoyable novel he shows us how an erotic novel is written not only by parodying the genre but by direct reference to it. This is Margot talking about erotic novels and their publisher:

> Let's face it—the thing that's unique about these particular books is that, for once, the writers have the liberty to deal with sex as frankly as they wish. If they do it well, they

accomplish something that's really significant: they throw a light on a very, very important subject that's always been a forbidden one for authors. If they don't do it well, then their books may be what a lot of people claim them to be—pornography. That's why, if you're writing one, I say you're justified in going to any lengths to acquire the material. . . .

Margot's definition of pornography as failed erotic art is probably the most useful explanation of that abused word.

There are a few other novels from the fifties worth noting before we conclude this chapter with a look at one of the masterpieces of erotic literature, Vladimir Nabokov's *Lolita*—the finest erotic novel published by The Olympia Press.

Two of these others are in the same satirical vein as Hoffenberg's novels: "Henry Jones's" *The Enormous Bed,* published in 1955, and *Stradella* (1962) by James Sherwood. *The Enormous Bed* is chiefly notable for its satire on upper-class English manners in the thirties, and for the quality of the author's prose. Whoever Jones is, his view of London society in that period is not much different from that found in the novels of Evelyn Waugh, who turned his contemptuous eye on the same years. There is a sequence in *The Enormous Bed* in which the narrator has an affair with the wife of the headmaster of his boarding school that is not only highly erotic but reminiscent of what Rudyard Kipling and George Orwell wrote about their early school experiences.

Stradella is a surrealistic, extravagant portrait of an aging Hollywood floozie. The narrator sees her from every angle and describes her with an archly humorous style.

It was my fortunate position to see her not only as Amourella, Goddess of Love, in a hurricane wrap-around nightie of misty-mysterious white stuff, chimera-like and cloudy, which was her blossoming costume on television, but also soggy and soapy in the bathtub with the water dirty and the sad suds soaking around her saggy breasts, slick with slop.

Stradella comes across as the kind of woman you'd rather read about than meet, and certainly not make love to (the novel is imbued with a discreet eroticism); but Sherwood's portrait of her is one of the most subtly drawn characterizations in modern erotic literature.

Deva Dasi and *Kama Houri* (1956), two novels about India by a Pakistani woman using the pseudonym of Ataullah Mardaan, are memorable for the author's ability to evoke India present and past. The Deva Dasi were sacred women who, like the temple prostitutes described in *Aphrodite,* devoted their lives to the fulfillment of the senses. The central characters are a mother and daughter who despite their sexual roles never see themselves as degraded because of the special relationship in India between sensuality and religion. *Kama Houri* may be described briefly as an historical novel about an English woman in India who learns about the country in a way that reminds one of Forster's *A Passage to India.* Mardaan excels in crowding her pages with the sights and smells of India, and her erotic descriptions are convincingly realistic.

The Whip Angels (1955) by Selena Warfield is one of Olympia's better historical novels. Set in 1866 in Victorian England, it is the story of what happens to an innocent young girl when she meets her cousins from abroad for the first time—a depraved brother and sister reminiscent of the children in Cocteau's novel, *Les Enfants Terribles.* They draw her into their deadly erotic games and force her to keep a diary of their activities. Decadence is delineated in a believable manner and the terror that is an element of eroticism taken to extremes is sharply conveyed.

In addition to the erotic novels mentioned in this chapter, The Olympia Press was responsible for the publication of a number of good books which don't fit into the genre, however bold their language or sexual passages. Among these are *The Ginger Man* by J. P. Donleavy, *I Hear*

Voices by Paul Ableman, *Watt* by Samuel Beckett, *The Black Book* by Lawrence Durrell, *Steiner's Tour* by Philip O'Connor, *Pinktoes* by Chester Himes, and *Naked Lunch,* by William S. Burroughs. It is interesting that in the history of The Olympia Press, whenever critics have undertaken to defend its publishing program, these books are cited, books which touch upon eroticism only tangentially, if at all—and the same critics have neglected the rich dark lode of true erotic literature published by Girodias.

Critics also cite *Lolita* (1955) by Vladimir Nabokov as one of the finest works of modern literature, forgetting that —first and foremost—it is an erotic novel of genius, and probably the best example of what can be accomplished when the limitless possibilities in the erotic situation are explored by a great writer. Nabokov himself has disagreed that the most accessible book of his later career is an erotic novel, and like all great works, it is in a sense beyond categorization. Nevertheless, the focus of *Lolita* is erotic: how else can you describe a narrative about a middle-aged man's obsessively passionate—and requited—love for a pubescent girl of twelve?

As Girodias writes of the novel in a recital of his difficulties with Nabokov entitled "A Sad, Ungraceful History of *Lolita*," Nabokov had written the kind of erotic story he had envisioned—like a kind of Platonic ideal form—but had never seen realized.

> . . . the story was a rather magical demonstration of something about which I had so often dreamed, but never found: the treatment of one of the major forbidden human passions in a manner both completely sincere and absolutely legitimate. I sensed that *Lolita* would become the one great modern work of art to demonstrate once and for all the futility of moral censorship, and the indispensable role of passion in literature.

Let us look briefly at the erotic aspect of *Lolita:* how it resembles other erotic novels, how Nabokov manages to imbue his book with eroticism without ever falling into salaciousness, and how his theme relates to others in erotic literature.

The reader who remembers the summaries of the novels discussed so far will recognize without much difficulty the correspondence between them and the story of *Lolita*. A middle-aged European named Humbert Humbert is sexually attracted to pubescent girls—he calls them "nymphets"—as a result of a lost childhood love; although he has aged, the objects of his passion must be the age of that first love. After being released from a sanatorium where he was treated for melancholia and "a sense of insufferable oppression," he goes to live in a small American town. He takes a room in the home of a loud, middle-aged woman he hates and discovers her twelve-year-old daughter, Dolores—Lolita, whom he worships on first sight:

> . . . from a mat in a pool of sun, half-naked, kneeling, turning about on her knees, there was my Riviera love peering at me over dark glasses.
> It was the same child—the same frail, honey-hued shoulders, the same silky supple bare back, the same chestnut head of hair. A polka-dotted black kerchief tied around her chest hid from my aging ape eyes, but not from the gaze of young memory, the juvenile breasts I had fondled one immortal day. . . .

Infatuated with his new-found love and eager to be near her, Humbert marries her frowzy mother; when the mother discovers his passion and then is conveniently killed in an accident, Humbert begins a long journey across America with Lolita. He is a victim of a passion so overwhelming that he will do anything to satisfy it.

Obsession is, of course, one of the prime motivations for characters in erotic fiction. It causes them to go to any lengths—debasement, even death—to satisfy their needs. In erotic novels the story line is advanced by the protagonist's search for fulfillment of his obsession, and this rule applies to *Lolita* no less than it does to any other erotic novel. Finally, in comparing *Lolita* with other erotic novels, we must take into consideration its tone: in erotic fiction the emphasis in descriptive passages is always sensual. Every object, every emotion, is eroticized—and Nabokov accomplishes this masterfully in *Lolita,* in a style that is often achingly romantic, but never cloying.

In an essay called, "On a Book Entitled Lolita," published in the American edition of his novel, Nabokov argues that *Lolita* is not a "lewd book":

> Certain techniques in the beginning of *Lolita* (Humbert's Journal, for example) misled some of my first readers into assuming that this was going to be a lewd book. They expected the rising succession of erotic scenes; when these stopped, the readers stopped, too, and felt bored and let down. . . .

It is true that Lolita does not consist of a "rising succession of erotic scenes," nor does it resemble Nabokov's perceptive description of the typical pornographic novel:

> . . . in pornographic novels, action has to be limited to the copulation of clichés. Style, structure, imagery should never distract the reader from his tepid lust. The novel must consist of an alternation of sexual scenes. . . . Moreover, the sexual scenes in the book must follow a crescendo line, with new variations, new combinations, new sexes, and a steady increase in the number of participants. . . .

Like Steven Marcus, Nabokov would judge erotic writing by its lowest common denominator, the formula novel. Neither writer admits the possibility that erotic fiction may not be confined to the "crescendo line" formula, although most of the novels described in this book do not follow such a formula any more than *Lolita* does. These objections are justified where they are applicable, but they do not apply to novels like *The Woman Thing, Irene, Story of the Eye*—anymore than they do to *Lolita*. *Lolita* may be discussed within a variety of contexts, but its erotic element cannot be denied; it is simply one of the best examples of the possibilities of this kind of writing. It illustrates "the indispensable role of passion in literature" with greater artistry than any other Olympia novel published in Paris, and like them its focus is primarily sexual.

V

IN THE AMERICAN GRAIN

IN THE YEARS between 1926 and 1956 erotic literature flourished in France; unhindered by government prosecution, The Olympia Press and its French language counterparts Jean-Jacques Pauvert and Les Editions de Minuit enjoyed a freedom unknown to publishers in other countries. Then, in 1956, French authorities began a series of prosecutions of Olympia Press books which gained such momentum that by the early sixties Girodias was confronted with an eighty-year ban on his publishing activities, a six-year prison sentence and a sizable fine; every book he published—including *Lolita*—was banned as soon as it appeared.

By one of those coincidences that so often affect publishing history, the rigid censorship which had prevented the printing of erotic works in America since the early nineteenth century was ended for all practical purposes by the mid-sixties, when a Supreme Court decision opened the gates to the dam behind which erotic literature had been held for a century and a half. The legal particulars of these decisions are not important to our purposes here; the effect is. Suddenly, anything could be published in America, and the country was flooded with crude factory-made pornography. Of the dozens of opportunistic publishers who took advantage of this new freedom to publish, only one, Parliament News in California, demonstrated at least a token interest in encouraging a native erotic literature by publishing its Essex House line of serious erotic novels.

For years Grove Press in New York had been the only American publisher to insist in court on its right to publish erotic writing; starting in 1959 with the first unexpurgated edition of D. H. Lawrence's *Lady Chatterley's Lover,* Grove published and defended in the courts *My Secret Life, Naked Lunch,* and the works of Sade and Henry Miller. When Girodias moved The Olympia Press to New York in 1967, he joined Grove Press and Essex House as one of the three publishers in America to insist on standards of literary competence in the publication of erotic writing. The stage was set for the first appearance of an American erotic literature.

Unlike French erotic writers, American writers had almost no indigenous tradition to draw upon. Until the sixties American censors had been so effective that it is only possible to name a few books and note a few trends before exhausting the subject of an American tradition in the genre. We remember, for instance, the story that Benjamin Franklin enjoyed collecting erotica, and was the first American to own a copy of *Fanny Hill;* we remember Mark Twain's clandestine forays into the field, "Some Thoughts

On The Science Of Onanism," and *1601;* we know there were a few counterparts to Victorian erotica, such as *The Memoirs of Dolly Morton,* a novel about a young girl's abolitionist efforts during the Civil War; the remainder of the works available are either trashy, like *M. Fontaine's Establishment,* or collections of jokes about sex, like those collected in *Anecdota Americana.*

Fearful of censorship, American writers did not write specifically erotic novels. Instead, they attempted to insert bedroom scenes in mainstream novels. Thus the erotic element in twentieth-century American literature is contained in a few passages in a few novels by almost every notable American writer, from Erskine Caldwell through Norman Mailer. Bestsellers like *Forever Amber* were expected by the public to contain just enough sex to make things interesting, but not enough to be shocking. This trend continued to accelerate into the sixties; books like *Peyton Place* seemed to sell in proportion to the number of elliptical sex scenes they contained. The novels of Irving Wallace and Harold Robbins continue this tradition. The reading public was definitely interested in literary descriptions of sexual activity— so long as the treatment of the subject was reasonably discreet.

It was as if sexuality had to be sneaked into fiction by the back door. The only alternative was equally hypocritical: suggestive novels in which the plot and characters revolved around a sexual situation but in which specific descriptions of eros were eschewed. This "soft-core" eroticism flourished in the fifties, when paperback publishers like Pyramid, Beacon, and Midwood specialized in suggestively salacious fiction by writers like Jack Woodford and Orrie Hitt, whose book *Hotel Woman* (1959) epitomizes this branch of the genre. *Hotel Woman* is a novel about the opportunistic manager of a Catskill resort hotel and the women he manages to bed. Hitt went a little further in his descriptions of sexuality in *Hotel Woman* than other soft-core writers, but the clichés are perfectly representative, as in this scene.

> He pulled off her shorts and threw them on the floor beside the bandana. She lay naked on the bed before him. Her body convulsed with desire. Hurriedly he undressed and lay down beside her. . . .
> "Take me, Al! Take me!"

Soft-core eroticism is distinguished from true erotic writing by its sentimentality and its respect for the social conventions. It does not enlighten, nor does it threaten the reader. As the critic Peter Michelson writes in *The Aesthetics of Pornography,* soft-core eroticism is the opposite of hard-core—or erotic literature as we have discussed it.

> "Soft-core" pornography evades threat and fear both by sublimating the primitive energies that are their source into socially approved activities. . . . Thus "soft-core" pornography flirts with animality, but does not descend into the naturalistic depths of its mythos. . . .

Literary sex, before 1966, was mostly divided in America between one kind of suggestiveness and another. G. P. Putnam's, after successfully publishing *Fanny Hill* in 1963, came out with the first hardcover edition of *Candy* just as Girodias was establishing The Olympia Press in New York. Various pirate publishers were taking advantage of the holes in American copyright law to issue reprints of almost all of the novels he'd published in Paris in the fifties. He had to start fresh, with new American writers he presumably hoped would be the equals of Trocchi, Daimler, Hoffenberg, and company.

He began slowly by republishing many of his old successes, but by 1970 an anthology of new Olympia writers bore testimony to the fact that American writers, despite the lack of a native tradition to nourish them, possessed a vision of eros that was both innovative and energetic. Like the

Olympia writers of the fifties, many of them used satire as a vehicle for comments on sexuality within American society: Ed Martin, Jett Sage, and George Kimball are part of this group. Others, like the poet Diane di Prima, wrote erotic autobiographies, or disguised their life histories in fiction. A large number of the new Olympia writers employed a surrealistic approach that was introspective and even claustrophobic: Lela Seftali, Renee Auden, Barry Malzberg, and Deneen Peckinpah. A few—among the brightest talents—chose to write in a naturalistic narrative form: Marco Vassi, Angelo d'Arcangelo, and Clarence Major, among others. The list of new Olympia writers is a long one, so we will touch only briefly on the most important books of some of these writers.

The first Olympia novel to attract wide attention was a story about the hippie generation of the sixties in Provincetown, Massachusetts, called *Barbara* (1968). The author, poet Sam Abrams, published *Barbara* under the pseudonym Frank Newman. The title character is a twelve-year-old girl who comes to a guru-figure named Max for her sexual initiation. Max is a strongly conceived Svengali figure who in the first chapter rapes a young couple he sees making love on the beach. Like Barbara they become his disciples, joining him in a series of powerfully described orgies. Newman's characterization of Max as a teacher—not only of sexuality, but of how to live the best life—is an instance of a recurring motif in erotic writing: the erotic artist as teacher. It is a theme which is most powerfully developed in the novels of Marco Vassi; we will return to it in a later chapter.

The problem with *Barbara* is that it is too episodic to achieve any kind of unity, or to make any point other than the obvious one that free sexuality was a major element in the hippie movement. As an erotic portrait of that generation, *Barbara* is of some value, and Newman's vivid sex scenes are excellent; but when he strays into politics or attempts to create characters other than Max, the reader loses interest.

What Newman lacks is a sense of humor in *Barbara*, a deficiency that is more than made up for in the work of Ed Martin. His first Olympia novel, *Busy Bodies*, appeared in 1963, followed in 1968 by *Inch by Inch* and then *The Masterpiece* and *Frankenstein '69* in 1969. Martin's novels are refreshingly vulgar fantasies in which the action moves with the speed and humor of a burlesque comedian's monologue. *Busy Bodies*, a novel that opens with an hilarious scene at a seance and which employs a cast of characters who are buried in coffins in a cemetery, remains his funniest book.

Crazy Wild and its sequel, *Crazy Wild Breaks Loose* were published in 1968 under the pseudonym of Jett Sage. The two novels possess an almost satanic energy. Full of sex and violence, they read like a Hell's Angels version of Kerouac's *On The Road*. The protagonist is an exaggerated version of Kerouac's Dean Moriarty who gets himself into absurdly violent scrapes as he travels by car and motorcycle across America. The author doesn't slow his roaring narrative once to allow for reflection on the part of his characters; they carom off each other like the moving parts in a pinball machine.

Poet George Kimball's *Only Skin Deep* (1968) is an equally energetic comedy about a midwestern high school, narrated in the first person by a teen-aged heroine more wide-eyed than Candy. Kimball's sex scenes are superficial but arousing, although his use of Eastern sex manual techniques as a preface to each scene is a tiresome device. Worse, however, is his tendency to employ satire as a bludgeon rather than a cutting tool, which is one of the weaknesses of Olympia satire. The new generation of Olympia satirists used the erotic novel as a vehicle for criticisms of their society, unlike the writers of the fifties who satirized the erotic situation itself.

Autobiography provided the new Olympia writers with a framework more conducive to reflection and the analysis of the erotic life than previous writers who had carefully separated themselves from their published fantasies. This first generation of American erotic writers was less afraid of being caught posturing naked before its mirrors. Diane di Prima's execrably titled *Memoirs of A Beatnik* (1969) is at its best and its worst when the poet describes her erotic adventures with literary figures of the fifties like Jack Kerouac and Allen Ginsberg. Her *Memoirs* relate the story of a young Italian girl from the kind of large immigrant family in which the older women gather around and pinch a young girl's newly developed breasts. She is a virgin, a budding poet, who at the age of eighteen discovers New York City and falls into the company of the beatnik *avant-garde*. The book describes her lovemaking with Kerouac and Ginsberg as if it were a kind of literary initiation, and it ends with her pregnant with child and a burgeoning literary reputation. What di Prima creates is a self-portrait of a new kind of woman, pre-women's liberation, similar to the self-portrait by Harriet Daimler in *The Woman Thing*.

Mary Sativa's *Acid Temple Ball* (1969) is a fictionalized autobiography that reminds one of di Prima's book because of its depiction of the hippie drug culture in the East Village of the sixties.

Sativa is less reflective than di Prima, but also less self-conscious about her sexuality. In *Acid Temple Ball*, she has an exact eye for details, the accumulation of which creates, in a breathy, ingenuous narrative, what is perhaps the most accurate, and certainly the most sincere picture in erotic fiction, of the hippie subculture of her time and place. Her attitude toward her own sexuality is one that is shared by most of the new Olympia writers, and radically different from the attitude of the writers of the fifties. They still believed, like Bataille, in erotic experience as a means to a spiritual end. Sativa, in the following paragraph, sees it as an end in itself.

> Man, my tender hippie flesh is for anyone with the cool to share it with me, but I'm totally turned off by impotent advertising executives who just haven't learned it's no big thing. If you're too terrified of life and love and the earth to fuck me, just lie in the dark and groove on being flesh, on feeling desire because another human being, a strange and unknown human being, is naked and open to you. I just can't put up with the masculine performing art of sex; I'd rather get high and hold hands with a hippie any time.

The naturalness of this philosophy is charming, if naive, in its lack of perception of the power of eros. Sativa's view is that sex is a natural function like other natural functions; more pleasurable than most, so it is performed more often, but by no means a path to deeper perceptions about the nature of the self and God. The logical development of this vision of sexuality might spell the end of artistic erotic writing, but the inherent mystery of sexuality is apparently as necessary as religious mysteries to the complicated psyche of the race. Civilization itself opposes the view of sexuality as a natural function. Even the new Olympia writers are unable to persuade us—despite protestations like Sativa's—that sexuality is as simple as all that.

Another disguised erotic autobiography, *Colors Roar By* (1969), published under the pseudonym Alexander Reck, questions Sativa's position. The protagonist is a writer of illiterate pornography who is constantly comparing his fantasies with the realities of his sex life. After commenting on the plethora of available sex newspapers and cheap erotic novels, he wonders if there isn't more surface than substance to the sexual revolution.

> Man, like everybody was obsessed. The clothes, the chicks falling over themselves to be as sexy as possible. It was

a massive plot. He was freaking out. Must be more to it. He was getting the best fucking he could ever imagine, all sorts of freaky practices, and it was boring him. If he could only understand the meaning of it all. He suspected that the emphasis on sexuality wasn't necessarily a sign of freedom, if people were really into their fucking, into nakedness, they wouldn't have to package it like soap.

Like *Acid Temple Ball, Colors Roar By* is a very young book with a meandering, episodic narrative. But the sexual action in both books is described with sufficient heat that the reader is able to ignore a certain carelessness of language.

It is doubtful that Sativa or any of the new writers perceive the contradiction between their "natural" attitude toward sex and their vivid descriptions of erotic acts, descriptions which focus on bodily parts with a voyeuristic enthusiasm. They linger too long describing nipples and buttocks and thighs, they lavish too many inventive adjectives on the human body, for us to take their professed "natural" attitude seriously. Erotic writers must arouse the reader's interest in what is happening on the page—and that calls for a literary transformation of the body into a sexually meaningful object of desire. Hard as they try, they can't escape this basic obligation to complicate what they would prefer to keep simple.

The Olympia writers who chose to write fiction rather than autobiography understand this obligation better. They use a variety of formal devices, but their narratives all display the good erotic novelist's ability to tell intelligent stories of passion. Orson Durand's *Angel in the Flesh* (1969) relates the adventures of a very precocious fifteen-year-old girl named Rosamund Kitteridge in the form of depositions given in court as part of a hearing on whether or not she should be placed in a private mental institution.

Rosamund is a modern girl who knows what she wants, and how to get it. She is sophisticated, unselfconscious, described as a genius by others, and the opposite of Candy:

she doesn't get taught, she teaches. She introduces dozens of men from sophisticated Parisians to Massachusetts state troopers—even her own father—to her kind of sexual freedom. She's self-confident, always in control, cool, fearless; to her, men are simply different experiences through which she can test her own erotic feelings. Next to Rosamund, Lolita, Candy, and Barbara are ignorant kids; one of the faults to be found with the character is that she is *too* sophisticated. Yet the author by his skill in creating different voices—so that a composite portrait of Rosamund is arrived at—almost manages to make her believable. Durand ranges from literary Paris to Vietnam, but from every point of view Rosamund is most convincing as a character when she is having sex. But what is she after? What is the point of Rosamund's erotic adventures? She tells the French master at her boarding school, "I fuck, therefore I am." When he asks her what she really wants, she replies: "To taste in my mouth my own life. . . . I want to make the world present to me."

Despite her intellectual and artistic abilities, Rosamund is the perfect male fantasy figure (although for that matter she is not a bad female fantasy, since she is always in control) because she defines herself by the sexual act. Of course she is not singular in this respect: her existential choice echoes similar choices by other characters in erotic fiction.

Vickie, the title character of *Victoria Welles* (1969) by Stephen Solomita, might be Rosamund's twin. Her obsessiveness about sexuality goes a step further, however—into a nihilistic attitude not only toward outsiders, but to her sex partners. In many ways, she is as frightening a creation as the character of Alex in *A Clockwork Orange*. From the beginning of the novel, when she is found lying in bed masturbating while her parents are overheard complaining about her behavior, to its end, when she is thirty-six and complaining about her own son's misbehavior, Solomita depicts a woman motivated solely by her erotic appetites. Sent to a special school for problem children as a teen-ager, she escapes being assaulted by black hoodlums by having sex with them; later when one of these friends wants revenge on a woman who has insulted her, Vickie joins in beating the woman to death.

Solomita is unrelenting: his portrayal of a modern maenad is violent and assaultive, his prose is hard and matter of fact. (He is one of the better prose writers of the new Olympia authors.) His view of the society through which Vickie moves in predatory fashion is flatly contemptuous. Vickie is an animal satisfying basic drives in a world full of other animals doing the same thing.

Two novels by Jon Horn, *Bondage Trash* (1968) and *Doctor Onan* elaborate upon this idea. In Horn's books the vision of sexuality as predatory animality is exaggerated to comic proportions by his satiric descriptions; his tone mimics the gossip columnist reporting with arch hypocrisy on the sordid activities of a sexual subculture. In *Bondage Trash* Horn employs surrealistic disorientation to express a vision of the world that is neo-Sadean. In the introduction to *Bondage Trash* he writes with acid tongue-in-cheek about a future in which:

> Gentle society where daily newspapers record atrocity. If there is any future, day by day the grim toll mounts. Children named and maimed: hapless and helpless victims raped by frightened girls in dark alleyways, and hideously mutilated by knife-wielding madmen. Acts of cruelty?
> We are offered a shining surface at all levels. . . .

Throughout the book Horn offers us a "shining surface," a collage of unrelated sexual episodes which seem designed to demonstrate to us how artificial and complex are the manifestations of eroticism. The narrator, pretending that his work is factual documentation of bizarre sex practices, describes himself as an average man.

> I am the fellow next door. It all started when I answered

an advertisement in a magazine available to every man and woman in the United States. Yet you will never read them, the reports on those who allow themselves exotic lustfulness and shuddering disgust in unusual friendship clubs for unusual people, adventurous, uninhibited, broadminded, intellectual, and cultured people. . . .

Horn's sardonic sense of humor and desolate view of the world, expressed in expertly parodied platitudinous language, is reminiscent of William Burroughs' *Naked Lunch,* down to its end in the stream-of-consciousness babble of a monologue entitled "Last Words Of X."

Bondage Trash is, in a sense, a very pure work: its satire is savage and unqualified, and its form makes no concessions to the demands of story. Those who go to it with the expectation of being aroused by its sexual content will be disappointed. Horn's second book, *Doctor Onan,* reads almost like a popularization of *Bondage Trash:* the subject is once again what psychologists categorize as "sexual deviance," but this time Horn tells a story of sorts, about a "sex doctor" named Doctor Onan, his adventures and his patients. One of them is Hector, a Puerto Rican pimp who pours his life history into the voyeuristic doctor's ears; another is the Countess, who is going through a phase of having sex with animals. In Horn's books people are never less than bizarre or more than ridiculous, even Doctor Onan, who attends ritualistic sadomasochistic performances in a mental institution, and visits an exclusive bordello so he can be beaten by tough lesbian bikers. In the latter scene he builds up to a description of his beating and then stops, to provide the reader with a catalogue of his world.

> Allow me to spare you the gory details, sensitive as I am to the fact that there's already a surfeit of sadomasochistic shenanigans in this repetitive chronicle of horror and obscenity, bestiality, voyeurism, miscegenation, incest, tribadism, floggings, tortures, group grope, murder, mayhem, things and stuff . . . and there's more to come. Don't go away!

The plot of *Doctor Onan* goes nowhere, despite Horn's attempts to sew his episodic narrative together, and eventually it just fizzles out in a topical adventure in which he and his boy slave hijack an aircraft and force the passengers into participating in an orgy. Although both of Horn's books deal with the same material in almost the same tone, *Doctor Onan* fails—even as a popular retelling—to the extent that *Bondage Trash* succeeds.

Horn's most striking accomplishment in *Bondage Trash* is the creation through the "shining surface" of style of an erotic work which is as abstract as a poem. Poetry, like painting since Cézanne, is no longer required to "mean" anything. It may simply *be,* its aesthetic appeal contained in its surface beauty; *Bondage Trash* is one of the closest approximations to an abstract erotic novel in modern literature, a work of lurid beauty fashioned from unlikely materials.

A number of new Olympia novelists write well-constructed stories on a popular level which—like the novels of Marcus van Heller in the fifties—display narrative talent while evidencing no more artistic ambition than is required to create a well-done fantasy.

C. S. Vanek writes novels in which women dominate and humiliate men, a reversal of the usual situation between the sexes found on the lowest levels of erotic fiction. Although his plots are contrived, his contempt for males seems sincere, lending a strange power to novels that are essentially lacking in substance. Both *Hide and Sex* (1969) and *Thrust* (1969) express this contemptuous attitude, but in *Hide and Sex* it is at the service of the story, and in *Thrust* the story is at the mercy of the theme.

Hide and Sex begins conventionally enough. Chuck Adams is a high-powered investigator in the field of industrial espionage. One of his clients, Wanda Tredgold, is the female head of a multi-million dollar business empire. Chuck's male aggressiveness is no match for his client's effortlessly domineering manner, and when she assigns him the task of finding her runaway male slave on their first meeting she easily reverses the traditional balance of power between male and female characters in erotic fiction.

Vanek is an expert entertainer, who specializes in scenes of male sexual humiliation and sex role reversals. As the plot of *Hide and Sex* develops, Vanek leads his characters through a bewildering sequence of sex changes which effectively erases their sexual identities.

Thrust is spoiled by a transparent bitterness in the depiction of its male characters. Vanek tells the tale of Sonia Trimble, the naive child of a strict mother who beats her for every infraction of her fundamentalist rules, a child who grows up to marry a husband who is even more cruel to her. The husband's piggishness grows apace from the first seduction scene in which Sonia notices the dirt between his toes and the thick hair on his body to the point at which he becomes involved in the world of sadomasochism and uses whips and chains on her. The other men Sonia meets are just as unrelievedly vile, with the exception of one, who turns out to be a fool. Vanek dwells agonizingly on the brutality of the male and the victimization of Sonia, who eventually finds happiness with a lesbian couple who have the only good marriage she knows of. The problem is that in order to convince us of the utter awfulness of his male characters, Vanek has made Sonia so stupidly naive she is not a credible character.

One of the most adept Olympia entertainers is an American poet who published only two erotic novels, both under the pseudonym Tor Kung: *My Mother Taught Me* (1963) and *Forever Ecstasy* (1968).

My Mother Taught Me has earned a word of mouth reputation as one of the most erotically stimulating modern novels; the author apparently set himself the task of writing a smooth, sensuous entertainment unadulterated by thematic concerns. Two elements set him apart from the other

Olympia entertainers: the quality of his prose and his absolute concentration on erotic details. Other novelists write sex
scenes separated from each other by the exposition called for
in their story lines. Kung moves his narrative solely by sexual
devices, while effortlessly managing to keep the reader's attention from straying.

My Mother Taught Me is narrated in the first person by
an orphan named Lars, who is fourteen when he is adopted
by a wealthy Swedish family. Because of some mysterious
scandal in his past, Lars has not been exposed to beautiful women since the age of seven, and when he is brought
into the Brahe home in Stockholm he is overwhelmed by the
sight of his stepmother's and stepsisters' bodies. They tease
him with glimpses of their breasts, and he quickly becomes
first a voyeur, then his older sister's lover, before ending up in
mother's arms. The women eventually end up forming a
kind of family harem for the boy. After making love with
his adoptive mother and her two daughters, he reflects upon
his happiness.

> When I had regained my senses we were all lying curled
> on the bed hugging each other. The sun was bright outside
> through the windows. I was in paradise. A paradise of
> woman. The only paradise . . . . Everywhere I felt them
> against me. Their flesh, the sacred and holy flesh of
> woman. . . .

Kung's sensuous hymn to sexuality and womanhood is
seldom assaultive despite his graphic descriptions, nor does
it fall to the level of hack work despite its unwavering concentration on the sexual act. Each character in *My Mother
Taught Me* exists within a closed world in which lovemaking is his reason for being. For this reason the novel is
an excellent example of a purely erotic work in which the
sole "socially redeeming value" is the positive depiction of
sexuality.

Kung's second novel, *Forever Ecstasy,* is a lesser book,

flawed by a hackneyed plot and the author's attempts to provide realistic psychological motivations for his characters. The story concerns a young schoolteacher who can't control an irresistible urge to arouse her male pupils. When they sense her weakness they blackmail her into fulfilling her own secret urges. Kung's ability at erotic description is unparalleled, but judging by *Forever Ecstasy* he is at his best when he limits himself to a rudimentary plot and a small number of characters.

Although the level of these typical Olympia Press novels of the sixties is as high as books in the same category published by the same firm in the fifties, it is doubtful if any of the writers discussed so far in this chapter are on a footing with exceptional talents like Trocchi or Daimler. There is a rule of thumb which may be applied in the genre: the best erotic novelists are able to write equally well about other areas of life. That rule applies almost without exception to the history of the genre up to The Olympia Press writers of the sixties. From Apollinaire and Bataille through Trocchi and Daimler, good erotic writers have made equivalent reputations in other literary areas. But with the erotic writers of the sixties this rule was broken. With the exception of the poet Diane di Prima, whose erotic autobiography has already been discussed, and two writers whose work remains to be looked at in this chapter, both the average and the exceptional new writers have published solely within the genre. The reason for this may be either that these writers do not possess the ability to succeed in other forms of writing, or that they no longer feel the necessity to justify their erotic work by excursions into other literary forms. Whatever the reason, this latter attitude indicates that the genre has attained a status in the minds of its writers that it has yet to achieve with the general public.

The best new Olympia writers, those who publish only erotic fiction, apparently believe that eros is sufficiently important to serve as the central focus of their artistic vision.

What of the good but untypical Olympia authors who have earned reputations outside of the genre? To conclude this chapter without looking at the work of Barry N. Malz-berg and Clarence Major would be to neglect two of the most serious Olympia writers.

Barry N. Malzberg did a number of pseudonymous novels for Olympia, and four that he put his own name on: *Oracle of the Thousand Hands* (1968), *Screen* (1968), *Confessions of Westchester County* (1971), and *In My Parents' Bedroom* (1971). The first comment that begs to be made about Malzberg's four novels is that they are written in a kind of opaque style that hangs like a gauze screen over his descriptions of erotic events. His novels are ambitious and determinedly modern, with a cold humor reminiscent of Beckett and Pinter, and a surrealistic disregard for the logic of narrative.

Malzberg's characters in *Oracle of the Thousand Hands* and *In My Parents' Bedroom* are alienated Becketian figures, and so, to a lesser extent, is the moviegoing hero of *Screen*. *Oracle of the Thousand Hands* is ostensibly a "study" of a sexual psychopath named D'Arcy written by a friend. The story is related in D'Arcy's voice, which is disdainful and cruel as he talks about his sexual experiences. At the conclusion of his story, following his admission that he has brutally murdered a woman, the author stabs him in the temple with a fountain pen. However, even this act arouses no emotion in the reader, because the novel has been related in such a chill, dream-like tone that it is impossible to feel anything for the characters: they are repellent, these images of us in our sexual lives.

The hero of *Screen* is a welfare worker who is addicted to movie viewing. Like Walker Percy's protagonist in *The Moviegoer*, Miller finds in films a means of extending the range of his own fantasies. Miller goes a step further than

Percy's protagonist, however: he steps through the movie screen and enters the lives of Elizabeth Taylor, Richard Burton, and Sophia Loren, conversing with them about their problems and even making love to them.

Despite melodramatic incidents the world created by Malzberg in his oiled, neutral prose is curiously affectless. It is also claustrophobic, both in its physical details and in the psychology of its denizens. *In My Parents' Bedroom* is an excellent example of the claustrophobic nature of Malzberg's fiction. Malzberg's narrator Michael Westfield joins a guided tour of his childhood home, which has now become a museum. On the tour he meets a mysterious young woman with whom he may or may not have slept; she becomes his companion in erotic play and in a dialogue which unfolds the nature of his response to his past.

Malzberg's fiction reaffirms the role of mystery in the erotic life. Like some of the French surrealists, Malzberg communicates the mysteriousness at the heart of the erotic experience and is able to persuade us of the importance of his exploration of these mysteries. Yet the vacancy at the center of his erotic novels belies the importance of this quest, effectively numbing the reader's mind instead of exciting it.

Poet Clarence Major's novel, *All-Night Visitors* (1969) is one of the few sixties Olympia novels on a level with the work of Trocchi and Daimler. Sex for its protagonist, Eli Bolton, is a medium for the reaffirmation of his unique physical self and the expression of the pain he is undergoing in daily life.

> This thing I am, this body—it is me. *I* am it. I am not a concept in your mind, whoever you are! I am *here*, right here, myself, MYSELF, fucking or being driven to the ends of my ability to contain myself in the ecstasy her little red mouth inspires as it works at the knobby head of my weapon, or if I am eating this goat's cheese, the pumpernickel, drinking the beer I have just bought, or whatever I happen to be doing, I am not *your* idea of anything.

All-Night Visitors is composed of a series of tangentially related sketches about a period in the life of Major's protagonist that includes experiences in South Vietnam and on the lower east side of New York. Eli Bolton falls in love with one woman who is frigid, turns to others, suffers for it, and seeks distraction in sex with strangers. He wanders about New York City attempting to come to grips with his war experiences and his own identity, always turning to sex for expression and sustenance, in despair at times but always acutely aware of himself and the world around him.

Major's accomplishment in *All-Night Visitors* is not just the creation of a character who expresses through sexuality the frustration and rage felt by a black man in the sixties. What he does in *All-Night Visitors* is to bring a hard vision of social reality to the genre, not only in his powerfully convincing descriptions of erotic experience but also in scenes like the final one in which his protagonist buys food for a Puerto Rican mother and her seven hungry children.

In general, The Olympia Press novels of the sixties exhibit the astonishing range and variety of themes, techniques, and achievements of modern erotic literature. In autobiographical, surrealistic, naturalistic, and satirical frameworks, their authors created a mosaic picture—a "secret record"— of the nature of American sexuality.

VI

THE ESSEX HOUSE NOVELISTS

> Start building up a new erotic literature based on beginnings rather than anticipating the end.
> —DAVID MELTZER

WHILE THE OLYMPIA PRESS published the new erotic literature, dozens of other firms were cashing in on the public's appetite for pornography. For the most part, what these marginal publishers printed bore only a generic resemblance to serious erotic writing. In fact, there was only one other publisher of erotica in America to undertake a program as artistically ambitious as Olympia's. He was Milton Luros of Parliament News, Inc., located in North Hollywood, California.

Parliament News was the parent publisher of a number

of magazines and book lines—all dealing with sex—but only two, Brandon House Library Editions and Essex House, were devoted to serious erotic writing. In 1967, a young musician and book dealer named Brian Kirby was given the responsibility of editing these two lines, and the credit for their success must go solely to him. In 1967 foreign and classic erotic fiction began appearing under the imprint of Brandon House Library Editions. Olympia Press books of the fifties were reprinted with new comments by the authors, along with editions of Sade, John Wilmot, Chinese classics, and a wealth of similar material; production values—beautifully designed covers, good printing, and paper—indicated a strong commitment to quality in the publishing program.

Brandon House Library Editions made the classics of erotic literature available, but the contemporary writers published in the series were at best skillful entertainers in the Marcus van Heller tradition. It wasn't until Kirby initiated the Essex House line of serious erotic novels in early 1968 that Parliament News became the West Coast equivalent of The Olympia Press. In all, over forty erotic novels were published by Essex House in less than two years.

If there is one distinguishing feature that comes to mind when the forty-odd Essex House novels are considered as a body of work, it is a heady sense of liberation. Most of these writers *played*, in the most open-ended, experimental way, with the form. They came fresh to it, were not hampered by any restriction other than the obvious one of telling a story with sex in it, and so the books they produced strike the reader who senses a unifying tone in them as either exuberant or immature. If he feels this exuberance, he may also detect idealism at its base, an idealism that is moral and political in its vision of present and future American society. If, on the other hand, he finds these same writers immature in outlook and expression, the reason may be that the use they made of their freedom was insufficient considering the possibilities open to them.

Kirby's stated intentions in editing the Essex House line were to encourage poets to experiment within the genre, and to offer more established writers a haven for their occasionally produced erotic work. Among the poets to write for Essex House were David Meltzer and Charles Bukowski. A few established writers expressed interest in the opportunity, but of them only science fiction writer Philip José Farmer was actually published by Kirby.

Kirby's policy was to find writers he thought might do good work in the genre, and then give them their freedom. To ensure a high level of effort, he decided that Essex House authors would not be allowed to use pseudonyms. Soon handsome-looking paperbacks bearing the Essex House imprint were appearing at brief, regular intervals.

One of the first was David Meltzer's *The Agency* (1968), the first novel in a trilogy consisting of it, *The Agent,* and *How Many Blocks in the Pile?* Perhaps as important as the novel itself were some thoughts about erotic literature Meltzer added in the form of an afterword. Along with similar comments in his other novels, they constitute the first manifesto on the subject of American erotic literature.

He begins with the idea that one of the functions of erotic literature is to reveal America's secret life.

> America's secret life is revealed in its wars and religious tracts certainly as well as in its fuckbooks. The so-called fuckbook pop-sub-culture is nothing more than a record of dreams.
>
> Lovemaking is, after all, more than what a man needs or what a woman insists on. It is something confronted every second and something still, as our culture would indicate, unknown and unrealized.

"Fuckbooks" take as their subject the part of our lives that we don't talk about. The genre expresses the unsayable, recreates the original mystery, and does so at its highest in moral terms. Thus Meltzer describes his trilogy as "fierce moral tracts." In a later chapter we shall return to explore the implications of this statement, but for now it and Meltzer's other comments will serve as an introduction to the contribution made by Essex House novelists to American erotic writing.

If anything, the novels of these writers were even more stylistically and thematically varied than those of The Olympia Press writers in New York. Essex House published rather conventionally written novels on psychosexual themes, as well as fairly experimental fantasies, memoirs, short stories, comic novels, erotic science fiction novels, and a variety of other hybrids. The one characteristic shared by most of these novelists was a political orientation that revealed a determination to explore America's secret life. Directly or indirectly, the Essex House novelist is interested in dissecting his or her society in order to examine its forbidden organs for signs of disease. Unlike The Olympia Press writers, Essex House novelists were relatively uninterested in the creation of erotic fantasies. That is perhaps the only marked distinction between them, but it is an important one.

In discussing modern French erotic literature I noted some basic categories in the genre, placing them in a pyramid, with erotic masterpieces like *Story of O* at the top, formula work at the bottom, and serious work done within the conventions of the genre in the middle. Essex House novels fall generally in this middle area, but at this point our pyramid requires more elaboration.

What is needed is a distinction between "pure" erotic novels and the hybrid erotic novel that grafts an erotic vision onto a previously established form like science fiction or the detective novel. Both the top and the bottom of the pyramid—hackwork and masterpieces—are made up of "pure" erotic novels. Hybrids generally make up the middle category. This hybrid concept is important because so many Essex House novels mix the conventions of other genres with the conventions of erotic literature. The results are often startling.

Season of the Witch (1968) by Hank Stine is a case in point. Using some of the speculative devices of science fiction, Stine manages to create in this novel one of the few believable portraits in erotic fiction written by men of what it *feels* like—sexually—to be a woman.

In a California of the future, Andre Fuller chokes a woman to death while making love to her on drugs. He is brought to trial for his crime, but the court instead of condemning him orders a less wasteful punishment: he must become the woman he killed. Wisely, Stine does not elaborate on the obvious futuristic devices he employs; rather, he focuses on what it feels like when an aggressive male is suddenly thrust into a woman's body. His use of another genre's conventions becomes a means for the powerful expression of the theme of sexual transformation. The struggle between the male psyche immured within a woman's body and the female psyche that eventually emerges is related in the form of an interior monologue in the second person singular, which has the effect of forcing the reader to identify with the character's emotional upheaval.

Stine manages to extend this identification to his character's sexual encounters with men, depicting with painful accuracy how women are victimized in these meetings. Stine examines sex roles with androgynous neutrality, while at the same time insisting on the real distinctions between the sexes. Finally, however, Stine's approach is moral: do unto others as you would have them do unto you would not be an inaccurate statement of his theme, but by his use of a device from science fiction, he particularizes the Biblical injunction so that one person is put quite literally inside another person's skin.

Stine's effort to get inside a woman's physical being and sympathetically voice her reactions to the crudities of the men she gets involved with is essentially political, in the sense that he is revealing the secret life of America. The fact that that secret life is exploitative and brutal in many instances is at the center of his second novel for Essex House, *Thrill City* (1969).

In *Season of the Witch* Stine told his story in a form—the interior monologue—frequently used in modern fiction, but seldom in erotic novels. *Thrill City* breaks even further with the straight first or third person narration generally preferred by erotic novelists. *Thrill City* is a collection of fragmentary stories and unidentified wisps of conversation that is unified by an inadequate plot device ("the Master" of the universe observes humankind in its misery) and a powerful sense of compassion for a country in which people are becoming increasingly brutal and brutalized.

Like David Meltzer, Stine's vision in his erotic fiction is urgently moral. He is repelled by how we use each other.

> We use each other. Frightened and alone in the bone caverns of our minds we reach out to manipulate others. Not content to suffer, we create suffering. We are black with sin, and yet we move.

Thrill City is a horrific, phantasmagoric portrayal of an America in which sexual assault is a metaphor for the violent disintegration of society. Stine sees the destructive side of Dionysus emerging not from individual men—the Sadean angle—but from society as a whole. Sexual repression inevitably results in psychic explosions.

Both Stine's theme and his treatment of it are echoed in other erotic fiction, notably in Charles McNaughton Jr.'s *Mindblower* (1969).

Mindblower may be approached on a number of different levels: set in the Haight-Asbury of the hippie sixties, its depiction of that milieu is realistically comprehensive;

it is also apocalyptic in tone, excessive in every respect, satirical and surrealistic. Its debt to science fiction is noted by science fiction writer Philip José Farmer in his afterword to the novel.

> . . . *Mindblower* is a science fiction book. All apocalyptic visions are science fiction books, although not all science fiction books are apocalyptic. McNaughton presents us with a world of telepathy, evil stunted beings living under the roots of a tree in the midst of a great city and planning world takeover, a seemingly incredible but true underground league of hippies who metamorphose into policemen and vice versa, humans turned into hairy beasts . . . a whole population taken over and destroyed by mental means. . . .

McNaughton's hero, Jack Flasher, reels energetically from one incident to the next as if on one long acid trip; perhaps it is his cheerful craziness which weakens the novel's impact, or perhaps it is the plot itself (which turns about a sex drug) that is inadequate; whichever, the effect is diffusion.

Predictably, the most successful use of science speculative fiction elements in the Essex House series was made by Philip José Farmer in *The Image of the Beast* (1968), its sequel, *Blown* (1969) and *A Feast Unknown* (1969). Appropriately enough, Farmer had written the first science fiction story to deal intelligently with sex in a novelette called *The Lovers* (1952). *The Image of the Beast* provided him with the opportunity to write an erotic fable. Its protagonist is "a private detective with the face of Lord Byron" called Herald Childe. Immediately, Farmer serves notice that he is not only going to mix science fiction with erotic fiction, but will ring in detective fiction as well: like Sam Spade's partner in Dashiell Hammett's *The Maltese Falcon,* Childe's partner is murdered while on a case. His death has been recorded on film and the film sent to the Los Angeles Police Department. It shows Childe's partner being sexually mutilated by a man dressed like the Dracula figure in every vampire movie. Childe, like Sam Spade, sets out in search of his partner's murderers, and finds himself exploring the world of the sexual supernatural.

Farmer calls both *The Image of the Beast* and *Blown* exorcisms, and one supposes that what needs exorcising is the beast in man—the terrifying Dionysian destructiveness his hero encounters in the villains of his two Herald Childe novels. Above all, Farmer is a good story teller, and the plots of both novels resemble those of good pulp thrillers. His prose is spare and logical, recalling the tone of detective fiction more than science fiction, but when he shifts into more fantastic situations, the transition is smoothly made.

For these reasons *The Image of the Beast* achieves some rather startling effects. As the plot develops, the reader cannot help but be fascinated by Farmer's outrageously symbolic concepts. But interest, even toleration, runs thin with a reading of *Blown*. The sequel seems to emphasize the weaknesses of the original, and Farmer's inventions cross the line of credibility even for lovers of fantasy. He is then seen as a master of startling concepts: in *Blown* it is a snake-like creature that lives in a woman's vagina. His *outré* imagery is not sustained, unfortunately, and most of his characters are like the two collectors of horror movie artifacts who figure in *Blown:* good ideas, but not living people. Intelligence and a vivid imagination cannot compensate for the lack of believable people, even in fantastic fiction.

A Feast Unknown is a wondrous concoction: Farmer imagines that Tarzan is the son of Jack the Ripper, and Edgar Rice Burroughs' pulp hero is cast as the villain in a struggle with another pulp hero, Doc Savage, here called Doc Caliban. Once again a clever fictional conception, but interesting more as an idea than a novel.

Yet Farmer, despite the weaknesses of these novels, makes probably the best use of a classic science fiction approach to erotic fiction. Hank Stine's use of science fiction devices is more successful because he takes fewer risks.

Richard E. Geis' *Raw Meat* (1969) is an example of how a heavy-handed use of these devices may stifle any erotic content. *Raw Meat* is more of a utopian fable like *Brave New World* than it is an erotic novel, despite the fact that the principal device of the book is sexual. Geis posits a computer-dominated world of the future in which sex has been totally divorced from reproduction, where birth is not mentioned in polite conversation. This world is run by "Mother Computer."

> Mother controls the population by regulating births to deaths. Sex has been separated completely from what the ancients called family life, and from the pattern of . . . children . . . pregnancy and birth.

In *Raw Meat* Geis speculates on some interesting ideas concerning the teleological significance of birth to sexuality, but like so many science fiction writers he expresses his ideas through the mouths of cartoon figures. The best s-f writers at least substitute a certain emotional ambience for the lack of breathing characters, just as erotic novelists substitute evocations of physicality and sensuality for full psychological characterizations. Geis' people in *Raw Meat* are puppets, but his theme starts a train of thought about the symbolic importance of reproduction in erotic fiction and rushes it to a logical destination.

The implications of his theme ultimately seem more memorable than his fictional exposition of it: the causal relationship between sex and reproduction is implicit in the work of serious erotic writers, contrary to the opinion of critics who castigate the genre for its unreality. Granted, birth is not viewed as a possible result of sexual activity in the typical formulistic fantasies of bad erotic fiction, just as the biological facts of death are not dwelt upon in murder mysteries; but eroticism is a means, a path, rather than an end to itself in erotic literature from Sade through Bataille to many of the Essex House novelists. So while the question of reproduction as one of the consequences of the sexual act is seldom directly confronted in erotic fiction, its importance is implicit. We do not have to see an autopsy report to realize the importance of a death in fiction, or that death is a consequence of the act of murder. But rather than focus on the consequence mystery writers concentrate on the causative act of murder, as erotic writers do on the act of sex. The act of sex, or murder, contains more potential for the dramatic revelation of important themes than their issues, the importance of which the reader must assume.

The devices of speculative fiction are put to good use in Gil Lamont's erotic novel *Roach* (1969). Lamont's protagonist, Malcolm Wren, is a fuckbook writer for the government in Lamont's vision of the future. Depressed by the mechanical society which controls his existence, Wren turns to drugs and sex in order to escape.

"Fuckbook writer. Sure you are. Get all your sex out of the memory banks of a fucking computer. . . ."

Lamont's style is more "experimental" (Wren's voice is unpunctuated and uncapitalized to suggest inner desperation) than his protagonist's whining presentation of a rather conventional theme.

It may be that science/speculative fiction approaches are fruitful when applied to erotic fiction because both genres originate in fantasy. The influence of the one upon the other is problematical, but this much seems certain from the evidence of the Essex House novels: speculative fiction demonstrated a new kind of literary freedom to erotic writers struggling against the conventions of their genre.

The Geek (1969) by Alice Louise Ramirez is an extreme example of a tendency in Essex House novelists toward outrageousness. Shock, while its action depends upon the susceptibility of the reader, has always been an important element in the impact made by erotic literature; it is stretched to its limits in many Essex House novels, but in *The Geek* the central situation is so absurd even satirical credibility is lost.

The hero of *The Geek* is a rooster who performs in a circus act with a Geek, a man so dehumanized that he will bite off and eat the head of a live chicken for a paying audience. In broadly farcical tones the rooster narrates the sexual goings-on in his circus, describing them in terms which reduce everyone to the bestial level of the Geek. Ramirez succeeds in milking some laughs from the reader standing before her sideshow, but her satirical intentions don't come off because of the overwhelming absurdity of her plot situation. The situation has been used before, notably in *The Autobiography of a Flea*, but it has never delivered more than some charming and funny moments because it is no more than a gimmick, even in the hands of eighteenth-century poets. However, *The Geek* is more than one long chicken joke: the tone of its erotic scenes is cruelly embodied in the image of a Geek biting the head off the rooster. The erotic scenes are assaultive out of proportion to the satirical, almost whimsical narration.

Even those writers who worked within the tradition of literary naturalism took bold stances in regard to their subject matter. Such a writer is Jerry Anderson, whose novel *Trans* (1969) is the kind of "fierce moral tract" David Meltzer called for.

Trans is a novel about sexual identity. Its protagonist is a young writer named Gene Norstrom who has traveled to Mexico to work and to get away from a constricted marriage. In the small town where he has gone his sexual activity is limited to the local bordello, where he has found one prostitute who will satisfy his preference for fellatio. He is aware that he would like to play both male and female sexual roles, and in his room he dresses in women's lingerie and contemplates himself in the mirror.

. . . a warm human being tired of solitary fuck-yourself-in-the-mirror games, a human being who felt enormous yearning for other people, for their immediate presence, their thoughts, their needs and reflections as well as their sexuality . . . and whether they were men or women didn't really seem to matter much.

Gene Norstrom has his first homosexual experience with a Mexican taxi driver and afterwards becomes even more certain of his insight, sustaining it even through the homosexual rape that follows. His travels across Mexico and the United States correspond to the zigzag pattern of his sexual traveling between male and female roles. As his open sexuality becomes more firmly established, he begins to function better in every area of his life. Each sexual experience confirms the wisdom of his original insight. At the end of the book, after many adventures in America and Mexico, he returns to his wife and another woman, to create a relationship in which he can play both sex roles.

On an acid trip he is able to elaborate on his original perception about the fluidity of identity:

> He saw that sex was an immensely satisfying way of expressing not just one of those possibilities within him but that it provided a rich, many-leveled means of communicating any number of the personality variables which he found inside. . . . He came to realize that he had the RIGHT to use sex to express as many facets of his nature as he was capable of conceiving.

Using the subject of transvestitism as a starting point, Anderson creates a multifaceted character who is not only shown in the process of spiritual growth, but who is able to embody the author's speculations about identity. The sincerity of Anderson's tone, the almost proselytizing fervor with which he develops his theme, sometimes leads him into awkwardness, particularly of language; but it also forces the reader to take him as seriously as he demands.

Binding with Briars (1968) by Paul V. Dallas is similar

to *Trans* in its emphasis on another area of "deviant" sexuality: sadomasochism. But *Binding with Briars* takes another direction: rather than using sadomasochism as a base to explore more compelling themes, Dallas limits himself to the discipline of his subject matter. The result is one of the three or four American erotic novels about sadomasochism that treat the subject as seriously as *Story Of O*. The naturalistic, specific details Dallas uses to create his portrait of an advertising agency executive in the grips of an obsession do not in any way resemble Réage's elegant surfaces, but the psychology of masochism may seem less mysterious to the general reader after Dallas' novel.

His protagonist is John Handley. Assertively masculine, married, Handley's secret life with a dominant black woman would never be suspected by his employees or his wife. David Meltzer's idea that America's secret life is revealed in its fuckbooks is perfectly illustrated by *Binding with Briars*. (The novel's title is taken from a poem by William Blake in which he describes not only the action of repression on the psyche, but the censorious minds likely to condemn a man's "joys and desires.") Handley's joy and desire is to grovel at the feet of a sternly dominant woman who punishes him for the slightest infraction, at the same time symbolically cleansing him of the forces which prevent him from feeling sexual pleasure.

Handley is drawn as an average, middle-class American male, a man so bound by the mores of his society that he kills himself at the end of the book rather than continue the descent into his personal maelstrom. Even then, he wonders what his son will think about him.

Dallas' characterization of Handley is psychologically realistic and arranged in a traditional narrative format. The scenes between Handley and his black mistress are detailed and persuasive, but Dallas avoids arousing prurient responses in his readers by de-eroticizing the sexual action. He is more interested in clinical descriptions of his character's humiliation than in expanding the erotic potential of a scene. Thus *Binding with Briars* reads like a fictionalized case study in which the sadomasochistic impulse is rendered so powerfully the facts themselves achieve the effect of art, without its substance.

A different approach to the same subject is taken by P. N. Dedeaux in *The Nothing Things* (1969) and *Tender Buns* (1969). In Dedeaux's whimsical treatment, spanking almost comes to seem the delight Victorian authors claimed it was. *The Nothing Things* are sorority pledges happily undergoing a trial period of punishment at the hands of senior sorority members; in *Tender Buns* Dedeaux's spankees are normal married couples who share a taste for the whip. The satirical possibilities in each situation are evident, and Dedeaux makes the most of them. By making the assumption that sadomasochism is not a problem but a sexual pleasure, Dedeaux is able to approximate the approach of Victorian authors to their favorite sexual variation. The lightness of his tone is worlds apart from either Dallas or H. R. Kaye's Gothic vision of sadomasochism. Kaye's *The Maid* (1968), an eroticized Gothic thriller on the subject of S-M, is prefaced by his remarks on the genre.

> Writing erotica is, without a doubt, an art, and I might add that it is an art as demanding and difficult as the execution of formulated poetry. In the writing of erotica, one encounters many technical problems that are not present in the writing of other types of literature. Of course, only writers are aware of these particular difficulties, and it is to their credit that erotic novels of high quality are now being written. . . . This field has been avoided, inhibited and suppressed too long.

Unfortunately *The Maid* is not a good example of the new erotic literature, being instead a nostalgic recreation of

Victorian erotica written in "conscientiously artistic prose." Like Victorian erotica, it has a musty feel to it.

The quiet rooms in *The Maid* seem to exist in another century from the contemporary paranoia of Gary Bradbrook's *Get It On!* (1969). Bradbrook's protagonist wakes up one morning stricken with an unnamed fear. He can't go to work, and even when he calls his mother he reassures himself with a trick that it actually is her on the phone. By the end of his conversation with her he's decided that he is a rabbit.

> We—my brother rabbits and myself—are this way because we have been given a gift: constant awareness of nature's potential for violence and destruction. . . . Death, for us, is like an overdue dinner guest; we know he may show at any possible moment.
> That's why we fuck so much, and with such urgency. Each time we feel the call to flesh, it is as if the gunman death has a loaded .45 touching lightly on our temples.

Bradbrook maintains the mood he sets at the beginning throughout the book, but his denouement—the protagonist's mother is the cause of his fear—is unequal to the expectations he has created.

Barry Luck's *Gropie* (1969) is about the rock music scene. Regis is the lead singer of an acid rock group called "White Fire," and he could be any one of a dozen rock stars who live the lives of modern princes of the realm. When Regis is kidnapped by a gang of rock groupies, the plot loses its last bit of credibility, a victim of its own shock effects. With the shock effects however, Luck gives us the kind of narrative detail found in Marcus van Heller novels, which *Ravished* (1968) by Richard E. Geis, and *Sarabande for a Bitch* (1967) by Mickey Dikes, resemble.

Ravished is a straightforwardly naturalistic story about two outcasts from society, a prostitute and a male hustler. Geis' characterization of their relationship is one of the more mature sketches of people who make their livings by having sex with others. *Ravished* has a strong narrative pull, as does *Sarabande for a Bitch*. But Dikes has captured van Heller's hard tone as well; his tough poet, Dave Franklin, might have stepped out of a Dashiell Hammett detective story—as re-written by Groucho Marx.

Many writers of erotic fiction adopt a tough, *macho* tone for their narration of erotic adventures; it suits very few of them unless they mitigate it with a corresponding lack of self-confidence in their characters. The protagonist of *The Bitter Seed* (1969) and its sequel *A Sort of Justice* (1969) by Henry Toledano, talks tough (he makes terse notes in his diary) about a life spent in pursuit of sexual pleasure, but can't help sounding like one of Kafka's insect people. Toledano's hero is himself, and his self-portrait recalls more the desperation of the erotomaniac of *My Secret Life* than the Henry Miller of the *Tropics*. As Philip José Farmer points out in his perceptive postscript to *The Bitter Seed,* the key phrase in Toledano's 600-page revelation of himself is, "I was attracted to whores because I could dispense with love. Love means allowing the other person to grow." Both novels derive a kind of hypnotic power from the mass of de-tails Toledano includes in his catalog of sexual episodes, most of them as sordid and depressing as the protagonist is repellent. Yet his honesty makes for a curiously sympathetic history of a sexual psychopath, a modern counterpart of the writer of *My Secret Life*.

The Dealer (1970) by "Malcolm Spade" (Tony Cohan) is the story of a young advertising man who decides to reject his bloodless, materialistic life situation to become a drug dealer. His transformation is convincingly sketched, but in describing his new lifestyle the author makes him so success-ful that he has him rubbing shoulders with dozens of drug-using celebrities, and the rather obvious satire thereafter ex-plodes the expectations Cohan raises at the beginning.

Eleven (1970) by Roger Lovin is a rather poignant, deeply

felt story about a love affair between a three-hundred-pound man and an eleven-year-old girl. Sexual fantasies about children are not unusual in erotic literature, but Lovin avoids the issue of pedophilia by giving the child, Rebecca, the body and emotions of a mature woman. His protagonist's physical ugliness is an important ingredient of the story, but Lovin draws him with compassion. Very few other erotic novels besides *Lolita* project greater romantic love between such an unpromising couple.

A character in *Eleven* comforts the fat man with the observation that ugly is as ugly does, and that is the closest Lovin gets to psychological comment. Like Nabokov but without his art, Lovin creates a genuine love story out of unlikely elements. Unlike Nabokov, Lovin doesn't seem interested in dwelling on the attractions of pubescent girls; having conceived his grotesque couple and made their relationship emotionally involving for the reader, he pursues the Beauty and the Beast theme inherent in the story. At the end, the fat man reflects on the happiness of his relationship with Rebecca, realizing that it wasn't sex he had wanted as much as her innocence. They made a refuge for each other.

> Rebecca came to me as a retreat from a hostile world. She came seeking a respite from a ceaseless round of envy and lust and hatred that her perfection brought her. She came because she could see on my face the same mask she had to wear, the mask of self-containment. And because she could recognize my love of beauty, and see that I found beauty in her.

Lovin's achievement is to treat what might have been a grotesque situation with a sensitivity that is often lacking in other Essex House writers. Like them, he begins by startling the reader, but then he follows up that original shock with the intelligent development of his conception.

In general, the young erotic novelists published by Essex House are more like than unlike the young erotic novelists published by The Olympia Press. Their novels reflect a common belief in the goals of the youth revolution of the sixties, which also defines the limits of their enthusiastic political consciousness. If the Olympia Press writers were more sophisticated in their espousal of the possibilities of the new liberation, Essex House writers made up for their occasional literary gaucheries with a passionate sincerity. (This aspect of their work is so important that future historians may turn to the erotic novels of the sixties for the most accurate literary reflection of the youth mood of those years.) Their novels are flawed by conceptions too often dreamed up more to shock than to illuminate. But considered as a body of work they are the fresh, energetic beginnings of a new erotic literature.

VII

THE POET
AS EROTIC NOVELIST

> Poetry leads to the same place as all
> forms of eroticism—to the blending
> and fusion of separate objects.
>
> —GEORGES BATAILLE

THE PERCEPTION THAT each atom of existence is a piece in a greater pattern underlying life, a pattern which may be glimpsed at heightened moments, is essentially mystical. It is a theme which runs through the history of erotic literature, suggesting that—just as every poem is an illumination of heightened experience—good erotic novels are illuminations of the heightened experience of eroticism.

This heightened moment may occur as a result of different stimuli, including danger, drugs, great stress, and religious fervor, but the one universal cause is the sexual embrace. The literature of this experience is erotic writing.

The idea that all we will ever know of the universal pattern of being is apprehended during these heightened moments is difficult to argue rationally, but it can be expressed with overwhelming emotional logic in both poetry and erotic fiction, forms which have their primary effect on the reader's emotions. By a recreation of the details which led to the moment of heightened experience—of union with the pattern of being—poets and erotic writers hope to approximate the emotional impact of the moment itself.

The literary methods they employ to achieve this approximation are seldom entirely realistic. Realism in literature results from an attempt by the rational artist to make sense in a logical fashion of disparate material and emotional experience. But transcendental experience cannot be understood logically, and the pattern it reveals cannot be fully expressed in realistic terms. Therefore both poetry and erotic fiction are designed literarily along emotional, not rational lines. The aim in both is illumination, not verisimilitude.

Like contemporary poetry, contemporary erotic literature suggests the marvelous by means of allusiveness, fragmentation, and disorientation. The unfolding of mystery seldom flows in logical narrative fashion, coming rather in startling, momentary glimpses behind the veil between us and the universal pattern. The poet or the erotic novelist's acceptance or rejection of the formal conventions of his medium determines the manner in which he will relate his insight. Erotic literature is as likely as poetry to be experimental in presentation.

The way a story is told in erotic literature is most often determined by emotional necessity, whether this is specifically erotic or not. The poets who have written erotic novels have discovered in the sexual encounter and in the conventions of the genre the material for the creation of new dreams. Their exploration of its mythical possibilities and its relationship to dreams is often matched by a correspondingly elliptical, dream-like narrative.

Having noted some aspects of the basic relationship between poetry and erotic fiction, let us look again at the idea that good (that we are talking about the best erotic literature should be understood) erotic fiction is an act of celebration, like poetry.

What is being celebrated in erotic fiction is the moment of heightened consciousness that occurs during sex. But at the same time the erotic novelist is obviously celebrating the body. He insists that the path to heightened consciousness is through erotic activity; both his characters and his readers must be stimulated by a sexual situation before he can approximate the feeling of its heightened moment. In a similar fashion the poet attempts to excite the reader's senses by means of his diction in order to recreate the feeling of the heightened moment. The poet and the erotic novelist choose emotional rather than rational persuasion as their objective.

The danger of this appeal to the emotions is that in order to be effective it must draw from depths in the personality that have been kept secret, often a frightening experience. The internal censor that protects us from our emotions by keeping our secrets buried is the same force that dulls our receptivity to the sudden insights of poetry. But we must be prepared to grapple with that censor, and to learn from what frightens us.

These similarities between the essence and the methods of poetry and erotic fiction are more than superficial; they suggest the possibility of a new way of reading erotic literature, as well as a direction for the future of the genre. We might change some words in Robert Graves' definition of poetic function in *The White Goddess* ("The function of poetry is religious invocation of the Muse; its use is the experience of mixed exaltation and horror that her presence excites.") and be discussing erotic literature: for "the Muse" substitute "Dionysus," for "poetry," "erotic literature."

Perhaps these ideas can be illustrated by the examination of a number of erotic novels by poets. In this century erotic literature has attracted a host of poets who have recognized the correspondence between the two forms. We have mentioned Apollinaire as the first modern poet-eroticist, and shown how the narrative of *The Debauched Hospodar* is governed by the logic of poetry, with the effect that its assaultive eroticism has a liberating effect on the reader —the same effect poetry has. We have discussed the French surrealist poets who wrote erotic fiction after Apollinaire, and now it is time to describe the influence of some contemporary poets on modern erotic literature.

When Essex House began publishing erotic novels, it was with the aim that many of them should be written by poets. The second novel to appear in the new line was David Meltzer's *The Agency*, the first volume in his Agency trilogy. In this trilogy, Meltzer conveys a poetic vision in spare, allusive prose. He also uses techniques special to speculative fiction and satire, but their function is to serve this vision. As the novelist Norman Spinrad writes in his afterword to *The Agent:*

> . . . "The Agency" is clearly Meltzer's paradigm of society; a mindless machine of which we are all "agents," *including* those whom the machine supposedly serves. . . .

Meltzer's metaphor for the way we conduct our sex lives is extended according to emotional logic. Power is seen as intimately connected with sex, and The Agency is "a well-organized self-sufficient, sexual underground." In *The Agency* a young man is picked up by sexual agents and—like O—spends the rest of the novel being forcibly indoctrinated with The Agency's tyrannical precepts. Brainwashed, he becomes an agent himself, ready to propagate the fantasy of The Agency. In *The Agent* the satirical possibilities implied in *The Agency* are applied more broadly. Here there are two agents, one straight-arrow, Eagle Scout type named White and the other a hard-boiled old operative named Black. Meltzer's deliberately ambiguous portrayal of two agents who may or may not be working for the same agency is often reminiscent of scenes from the movie *Dr. Strangelove,* but his use of multiple first person narrative, voices sliding in and out of focus, confirms that his intention is to present his concepts in the indirect, allusive manner of poetry.

How Many Blocks in the Pile? only suggests the existence of The Agency; instead of confronting the subject directly, Meltzer creates an exaggerated portrait of its customers—a married couple who respond to sexual advertisements. It is constructed differently from *The Agent* or *The Agency,* but it develops the same theme. Spinrad's view, that in this trilogy "the Agency is both cause and effect of dehumanized sex and its relationship to American society" is a perceptive reading of Meltzer.

The poet's notion that erotic writing deals with the secret sexual life of America is abundantly illustrated by *The Agency* trilogy, but in his next novel, *Orf* (1968), he not only plumbs the national psyche on a deeper, mythical level, he achieves a fusion of poetic approach and erotic material that beautifully demonstrates how the lessons and concerns of poetry can affect modern erotic writing.

Orf is one of Meltzer's finest erotic novels. It will reward careful consideration by yielding beauty of language, complexity of concept, and an hypnotic vision of the nature of power and fame in America. Orf is a rock singer, a contemporary incarnation of the poet Orpheus. Meltzer has accurately perceived that rock stars have replaced movie stars in the national mythology, and that perception is the basis for his treatment of the narrative.

> All singers are incredible sex gods. The movie in her head tells her how it should be. She can own me for a moment or two and (thus) be transfused, transformed with the sperm of gods.

Here Orf is commenting on a rock groupie who has invaded his dressing room in order to have sex with the idol she and millions like her have created, only to find him impotent. A god must have his priestesses; teenaged girls act out this role for rock musicians, offering their bodies in exchange for a momentary connection with them. Aware of this, Meltzer calls groupies "Sacred Harlots."

In *Orf* he has structured his story like a poem. By doing so he achieves a prose narrative that has a greater flexibility than is usually found in conventional fiction. *Orf* begins with an "Epilogos" in which Orf's mother speaks of his death as the mother of a mythological figure might.

> Now they have him. . . . He is theirs as he always was, as it was his destiny to be. He was never his own. . . .

Orf is introduced in this section along with his agent, Schlink, a repulsive character who exploits singers in order to make enough money to "break out of time's prison" and prolong his life. In his view, Orf is like an amoeba, "There's always another kid, there's no end to them." Everyone gets exploited in life. But Schlink is far from a caricature of the greedy agent. He personifies Meltzer's theme of exploitation, but the poet allows him his own human meaning. So much so, in fact, that he often seems the strongest character in the novel.

Following the "Epilogos," in which Meltzer introduces his theme, the treatment of it, and his major characters, there is a long section consisting of numbered paragraphs and scenes called "The Eighty-Eight Hymns." Here Meltzer offers glimpses of the music world, Orf's monologues, and "raps" which are assemblages of news items, stories, radio broadcasts, conversations—a collage of sounds designed to reflect the verbal garbage of contemporary American popular culture. It is against this background that Orf's myth is told.

Orf himself is presented from different angles. When he is narrating in the first person, it is a poet's stream of consciousness that we hear, as in these lines:

> When I was a fucked-up grub of a punk kid crawling to and fro, on no fucking merry way, just a gray, tongue-tied, gloombag. . . .

Many of the sections in "The Eighty-Eight Hymns" make use of the formal innovations of modern poetry; the way snatches of conversation, advertising and news items blend into one another recalls similar designs in T. S. Eliot's *The Wasteland* and Hart Crane's *The Bridge*.

The story itself takes Orf to national prominence at a concert in which he is literally ripped apart by his "Sacred Harlots." Other musicians and disc jockeys appear briefly in Meltzer's descriptions of the music world, but he and Schlink are the most prominent characters, along with Orf's wife Esther, who is shown getting a secret abortion in wretched circumstances arranged by Schlink; she too dies at the rock concert.

Of course the story of *Orf* is a retelling of the myth of Orpheus; the rock singer is a closer equivalent to Orpheus than the modern poet, if only because of the violent nature of the audience's response to him. The story has been retold in other erotic novels, but never with the mythmaking intent Meltzer brings to *Orf*.

His problem was threefold: to retell a potent myth in modern terms, to portray the world of the rock musician, and to do so without neglecting erotic content. His integration of these elements is successful primarily because of the influence of poetry on his structure and language. This compressed, suggestive prose (illustrated by a line like "Hoodoo, voodoo bells attached to the door ring and chime a fast black mass tone-row") adds an extra dimension to the novel's treatment of the myth; it also demonstrates the verbal resources poets bring to writing erotic fiction.

Aside from the mythic elements of the story and its relationship to the nature of fame and power in America, there is the recurring theme of exploitation that Meltzer introduced in *The Agency* trilogy. Schlink is the embodiment of this theme, but it is summed up best by Orf's mother in a concluding "Logogriph": "We are used as surely as we use and in the end we are in a daze."

Meltzer seems to be saying that in America we use sex and dreams (the rock singer creates the background music for our dreams) to affirm the fact of our existence. We use them and then discard them when they have served us, and still our spiritual vacuum is not filled. Our emptiness leaves us in a state of dazed confusion and frustration, which often manifests itself in violence. Speaking of Orf, his mother says:

> What is the story, the song we crave and are always alert for? It is his story, the story of fame, the story of the hero whose fame is food for the millions. That they devour fame is immaterial. That is what fame is for.

Like Orpheus, Orf is torn to pieces. His fans hope that his "meaning"—the music which has created his fame—will be transferred to them by their possession of his flesh.

In contrast to the rich language of *Orf*, Meltzer's fifth novel, *The Martyr* (1969), is written in a flat style suited to the world of childhood. Jeremy and Rebecca are brother and sister. They play sexual games with each other, but their childish experiments are innocent. Then they're left with their Aunt Lorna, a repressed, religious woman who thumps the Bible with one hand while she arranges sexual tortures for her charges with the other. She is joined by relatives and other children in her insane mania, and Rebecca is horribly murdered in the last pages of the book. These scenes equal anything in Hubert Selby, Jr.'s *Last Exit to Brooklyn* in their powerful transmission of Meltzer's vision of thwarted sexuality.

Aunt Lorna's religious mania is destructive: she believes that she is the agent of God, and that her mission is to punish the guilty. Grotesque as she is, Meltzer makes her, like Schlink, a three-dimensional figure. Her progress from embittered frustration to murder is plausible in the detailed emotional context of the Christianity she exploits. In Meltzer's descriptions of her there is a lyricism which suggests that even within the stark outlines he has limited himself to there is a poet's mind at work. Lorna, standing in the bathroom, looks at herself.

> The cool air comes through the window open slightly by the toilet bowl. The cool air comes from within Aunt Lorna as she breaks wind in the water and shuts her eyes in modest shame. The cool air is the coolness of clouds that circulate in her empty womb. Clouds the texture of cotton that, in her mind, she tears apart with fingernails she no longer has.

Meltzer followed *Orf* with his most ambitious project, *The Brain-Plant Tetralogy* (1969) consisting of *Lovely, Healer, Out,* and *Glue Factory.* In classical Greek drama, a tetralogy is a group of four dramatic pieces, either four tragedies or three tragedies and a satire. Meltzer's Brain-Plant books are not tragedies in the classical sense, and satire is a prominent feature of each of them; but his extrapolation of tendencies in American society of the late sixties and their application in his prophetic fiction renders a tragic, scorifying vision unequaled for its ambitiousness in contemporary erotic literature.

Meltzer's tetralogy demands study as a whole, before it is possible to grasp the meaning of any one of the four novels. The complexity of his design, his fantastic inventiveness, and his large cast of characters are such that it is best to approach a critical reading of them with a few guidelines. Meltzer's novels are designed according to the imperatives of poetry, not logical prose fiction; he makes use of devices from speculative fiction; his tone is often satirical, but his novels are not satires; and finally, his overriding theme is the exploitation of people through sex, power, and dreams. His comments on the Brain-Plant books (from an author's note to *Out*) give us further insights into his method. He is talking about the final book. *Glue Factory*, in which he promises the following.

> In it, we knit together many of the lives & life-styles I've so randomly strewn about these pages. More outrage. More sex made more outrageous. . . . A dream-vaudeville flip-card book.

The word "vaudeville" is apt when applied to Meltzer's technique of interweaving dozens of different points of view in his narrative, but its connotation of entertainment could hardly be further from the mark when applied to his grim vision of the future.

Meltzer's achievement in the Brain-Plant Tetralogy does not lie in the creation of characters, because the people in the four novels are either deliberate caricatures or disembodied voices; nor does his achievement lie in the creation of a central fantasy. His projection of a future government ruled by "Military Industry" in which "Rads" (radicals) and "Rebs" (lower middle class whites), "Snarks" (sexual anarchists) and black militants are pacified by "Fun Zones" (ingenious Disneylands for the satisfaction of sexual fantasies) is simplistic—like R. Crumb cartoons, as Frank M. Robinson points out in his afterword to *Lovely*. Meltzer's achievement lies instead in the utterly convincing manner in which he argues his theme of exploitation. He takes hundreds of small set pieces of dialogue, erotic activity, and anecdotes, and builds from them, piece by piece, a mosaic which has the cumulative effect of showing the reader "the naked lunch on the end of his fork." By demonstrating in fiction how we are exploited, and what it is likely to lead to, Meltzer enacts the poet's traditional role as seer.

Lovely introduces Meltzer's vision of the future, and refers on its first page to the exploitation motif that will recur again and again in the tetralogy.

> The distracted consumer is the most vulnerable. Basic axiom. In times of social crisis, and these are times of such chaos, it's our job to create and develop new images, new products. The citizens, Rad or taxpayer, must have fun. Keep them distracted, off guard, and they'll consume until they're consumed and disposed of. . . .

Two leaders of "Military Industry/Christian America" are congratulating themselves on their control of the citizenry. Their "Fun Zones" have replaced social programs like Welfare, Medicare, Social Security, and Unemployment Insurance, as well as parks, museums, and libraries. They are able to keep the different factions of the populace distracted and divided by offering bread and circuses. The nominal hero of *Lovely* is an ineffectual poet named Arthur Goldwheel, perhaps the only sane man in a mad world; but Meltzer's satire doesn't spare him any more than it does the "Rads"—Meltzer's ironic view of the hippies of the sixties.

Healer's main character is a medicine man figure named Walker who works for the government. His job is to help a woman named Laura Golden Eyes, whose participation in erotic Indian rites in a previous life has made her unresponsive to sex. Walker is used by his superiors, and eventually even by the woman he is assigned to help.

Out is the story of a frustrated man lost in the complexities of "Military Industry/Christian America." He hates

the world he lives in, but he can't survive without it. Forced
to exploit his fellow citizens, he learns there is no way out of
the trap he's in.

Glue Factory brings most of the characters from the first
three Brain-Plant novels back for a final tour of Meltzer's
grim world of the future, and a new character is introduced:
God. Like an old vaudeville trouper, God makes some jokes,
and—in a final scene—is shown making love to himself. Significantly, in *Glue Factory* Meltzer the novelist comments—
within the narrative—on his intentions regarding the characters he has manipulated like puppets. One of his female
characters is revealed to have been, in the course of the
tetralogy, many women.

> Like all people in the series, her body and face are inter-
> changeable. . . . Part of the unfolding mystery is the discov-
> ery of all the faces one wears. . . .

The Brain-Plant Tetralogy is a multifaceted work of
great complexity—so much so, that it can only be described
obliquely. In a work of such ambitious scope, Meltzer could
not avoid some pitfalls. The satire which is the dominant tone
of the series is often simplistic; the devices of speculative
fiction sometimes ring hollow (like the synthetic womb introduced in *Glue Factory*); the caricatures are too broad; and
Meltzer's experimental techniques at times seem unjustified
by their results. Nevertheless, the Brain-Plant Tetralogy, because of the extravagant, entertaining, violent, prophetic
vision it conveys, is one of the high points of modern erotic
literature.

The theme of *Star* (1970) is once again exploitation; in
this case the users are Hollywood studio bosses, and the used
are both the movie stars who people the celluloid dream and
the audiences to whom they play. Meltzer implies that Hollywood manufactures our dreams as a people, and these film
dreams, like sex (and rock music in *Orf*) distract us from
noticing how we are exploited.

Alan Zephyr is a young movie star who wants to find his parents. A private detective named Musk is hired to aid him, but Musk—a seedy, sinister creation like Schlink in *Orf*—is actually an enforcer for the studio bosses who have bred Alan like a prize bull from birth. His parents, it develops, were also movie stars, and when he meets his father—an Errol Flynn type—he learns that the studio is using the former screen lover as a stud. His genes, combined with those of female stars, will create another generation of stars. They will be carefully nurtured, as Zephyr was, at a secret ranch where the breeding is carried out. Finally, Zephyr finds himself making love to his mother alongside his father, who says he's sired thousands of potential stars. "How does it feel to be a product made in a factory?" a reporter asks Zephyr's mother after her appearance on a late night talk show.

Star is, after *The Martyr*, Meltzer's most accessible novel. He seems to know as much about the film world as he does about the world of rock music, his satire is controlled and effective, his characters are three-dimensional, and his narrative is straightforward. Most important, his application of the theme of exploitation is perfectly suited to his subject. It is as powerfully stated in other novels, but never so directly as in *Star,* in which he satirizes—for our amusement and horror—the most public of America's dreams.

Meltzer proves in his ten erotic novels that he was correct in calling them "fierce moral tracts." Although his work is crowded with vividly erotic scenes, their effect is more often frightening than arousing. In his novels eroticism is at the service of his vision of exploitation: sex is the physical use of one person by another, and it is assaultive and outrageous, never loving and tender, never a path to anything else. In a sense, his eroticism is an indictment of sex because it usually involves the manipulation of others.

Poet Kirby Doyle's novel, *Happiness Bastard* (1968) recounts the day-to-day existence of a character named Tully

McSwine. Tully lives on New York's Lower East Side, where he drinks and pays court to his mistress, Dolly. Occasionally he writes poems, but mostly he talks about his life with his friends, literary figures from Beat Generation days like Allen Ginsberg. Nothing much happens in *Happiness Bastard* in the conventional sense, but Tully's jocular interior monologue creates a portrait of the poet that bears more than a passing resemblance to J. P. Donleavy's boozing clown, Sebastian Dangerfield, in *The Ginger Man*.

Doyle plays with the language like a child playing with his first set of finger paints. Sometimes the result is fresh and funny, but too often his meandering narrative lapses into pointless verbiage. The reason for this may be the lack of necessity in the novel: a writer may decide to eliminate conventional plot elements in his story, but if he can't find another way to introduce tension, the reader's attention will wander. *Happiness Bastard* is a frequently entertaining tour through a poet's mind as he goes about his business in the universe, but as an erotic novel it lacks direction or theme. Doyle's approach is summed up in one of Tully's reflections upon the nature of things.

> I neither demand mighty efforts of production from myself nor reject that which I do produce. I merely go out and walk upon the planet and look at the things scattered thereon. I look, and I like and dislike, but I change nothing, nothing changes.

What should be emphasized in regard to *Happiness Bastard* is its exuberant good humor, and the influence of poetry upon its language. Doyle interjects actual poems in the pages of the novel, but more striking are lines like "the sky crisp as chips and blue as meadows" and "The sidewalks dangerous from gesturing hands flying about my face in a frenzy of barter." Because of lines like these, and his cocky attitude, Tully is charming despite himself.

> & so the feather flies . . . depraved from the crib and

> no help for that. Years of thrashing debauchery seeped in
> behind my orbs. The bones of my cock clanked and ridged
> in unblinking expeditions. . . .

Michael McClure is a well known San Francisco poet and the author of *The Beard,* a play that brought him national notoriety because of its sexual content. His autobiographical novel, *The Mad Cub* (1970) was considered for inclusion in the Essex House series, but was finally published by Bantam Books. *The Mad Cub* is not, strictly speaking, an erotic novel; but it contains sufficient sexual content to justify its inclusion in a survey of erotic novels by poets. McClure's poetry, particularly his "Fuck Ode" in *Dark Brown* (1967) indicates that sexuality is one of his important themes.

The Mad Cub is McClure's *Sorrows of Young Werther,* the experiences of a young poet in Middle America. It is an agonizingly subjective, romantic portrait of the young poet and his friends that McClure creates, and he does so along the lines we have been discussing:

> Novels are written to show you that there is psychological sense to actions but there isn't—only soul reasons and spirit reasons.

Charles Bukowski, the author of *Crucifix in a Deathhand* and *It Catches My Heart in Its Hands,* writes ironic, often bitter poems about life's losers—horseplayers, drunks, petty criminals—and how they survive on the seedy, desolate underside of the American Dream. His prose is about the same world. *Notes of a Dirty Old Man* (1969) is a collection of his columns from the California underground newspaper *Open City.* Bukowski is an American Céline, fulminating against the slick dishonesty of American life from the angry, embittered, sarcastic viewpoint of a man who prefers living on the bottom. *Notes of a Dirty Old Man* is unrelievedly harsh in tone—Bukowski expects the worst and always seems to find it—and sex is accorded no higher status than any other activity.

Bukoswski's prose is a logical extension of his poetry; he is an excellent natural story teller, and when the subject is sex, his black perspective is perfectly suited to the portrayal of the kind of absurd tawdriness he is drawn to. His milieu is the seedy furnished room, illuminated by a naked lightbulb:

> the night the 300 pound whore came in I was ready. nobody else was ready but I was ready. She was god awful fat all around and not very clean either. . . . both being very drunk, we worked on and on, myself being thrown off again and again, but leaping back to battle. I'm sure we both wanted to quit but that somehow there was no way out. sex can sometimes become the most horrible of tasks. . . .

Although he sometimes finds a grubby tenderness in such encounters, Bukowski's customary attitude toward sex is disgust. For him it is simply one more piece of evidence in the case he argues against life: it is all a hopeless sham, a confidence game no one wins, and the best one can do is to recognize the absurdity, avoid being taken in, and drink a lot to kill the pain. For Bukowski, sex is a dirty joke of metaphysical proportions, although he would sneer at the suggestion that the subject is larger in its implications than a 300-pound whore.

But the subject of erotic literature is not only sexuality; if that were true the genre could well be dismissed as light entertainment. It would seem no more consequential than the romances adolescent girls read. There are two strains in erotic literature. One treats sexuality as an end in itself, and the other treats it as a path into the darkest regions of the soul. The first strain has produced some charming celebrations of physical love, and a great deal of conventional pornography. The other has given us works of art, like *Story Of O, Irene, The Story Of The Eye* and the books discussed in this chapter. Both have valid places in the genre, but there is a greater potential for the creation of serious literature in the second.

Detective novelists gain access to the secrets of the psyche through the act of murder, and erotic novelists get behind our civilized exteriors through the sexual act. Few of us commit murder, but most of us make love; which one of us has not been awakened to the existence of darker forces in us during the sexual act? Sex, like violence, is both a manifestation of these unknown forces and a confirmation that they exist. For a moment during a fist fight a man may feel coming from within an ability to kill he didn't know he possessed; a similar revelation may occur during sex, when all restraints are removed from his imprisoned psyche.

This moment—when the veil between our civilized selves and our primitive selves is pierced—is like a hole in our armor through which the erotic novelist slips to discover the nature of the secrets we have taken such great care to hide.

My contention is that poets who write erotic novels find the genre sympathetic because its subject matter is part of the raw material of poetry, and further, that since erotic novels are written along lines determined by emotional necessity, poets may write erotic novels the way they write poems. The poet who writes a psychological novel with a conventionally logical narrative does so with another part of himself than he draws from when writing poems. One kind of creativity is opposed to the other, which is not necessarily the case when he writes an erotic novel.

Poets have two sacred duties: one is to keep the language in good repair, and the other is the illumination of experience. In the performance of this second duty, poets have turned their attention to erotic writing. Mankind has been riding the crest of revolution for a long time, and revolution springs many doors. In the midst of social and psychological upheaval, sexuality has been brought out into the open for public examination. It is the poet's task to interpret and illuminate its meaning. He has his ear to the same inner music when he writes poems or erotic novels, and the full harvest of his interest in eroticism is still to come.

VIII

EROTIC POETRY

> The imaginative approaches to the theme of love, to the making of a mythos for it, are manifold, and poets in this artistic mode of the pornographic genre *are* poets. Their use of pornography, therefore, follows the dictates of imagination.
> —PETER MICHELSON

IF THE POET and the erotic novelist draw from the same well —and are often the same person—why is it that we do not have a distinguished tradition of erotic poetry? It might be argued that poets prefer to cast their sexual feelings in the more idealized (and acceptable) mold of love poetry—for a large number of good love poems have been produced in this century—but the reason may be more circumstantial. Censorship does not spare poetry when it sees a forbidden word on the page, and poets have a hard enough time finding an audience these days without running the risk of seeming offensive as well as obscure.

There is a dignity inherent in the tradition of poetry: it speaks to great themes in beautiful language. In addition, poetry must bear the burden of delicacy and subtlety that has been associated with it in the modern era. One would not expect to find a limerick beginning "There was a young girl of Pitlochry / Who was had by a man in a rockery. . . ." among the collected poems of T. S. Eliot. Yet the most popular form of erotic poetry is without a doubt the lowly limerick. Readers no longer memorize their favorite poems with the zeal of nineteenth-century readers, but chances are they've committed a limerick or two to memory in their lifetimes.

The English author Norman Douglas collected fifty limericks, most of them from what he terms the golden age of the limerick, the Victorian period. This delightful collection, entitled *Some Limericks,* was published in America in 1967. Those who believe that verse should be thin-blooded and portentous may recoil from the coarse humor of Douglas' limericks and his equally funny commentaries on them. The following is a good example of both.

> There was a young man of Belgravia,
> Who cared neither for God nor his Saviour.
> > He walked down the Strand
> > With his balls in his hand,
> And was had up for indecent behavior.

Douglas comments:

> This is the first limerick I ever learnt, at the age of ten; it has remained fixed in my memory. How many other things have been forgotten! I print it chiefly to show that even at this early period our absurd London street-regulations were already in force. . . .

The limerick—rhythmical, brief, and humorous—is the ideal form for erotic poetry in puritanical cultures. Sex in the limerick is put in its place by laughter. The limerick doesn't require the serious consideration of erotic themes; the sniggering of the school yard may be detected in its regular rhythms. Sex only becomes threatening when it can no longer be laughed at, for laughter implies that a safe distance has been set between the reader and sexual experience, whether the laughter originates in embarrassment or sophistication. This may account for the fact that most erotic poetry is humorous; generally speaking, when poets write seriously about sexuality the results are called love poems.

Verse forms, like laughter, put a safe distance between the poet and sexual experience, a distance the reader feels comfortable with. One of the masters of form in twentieth-century poetry is the late W. H. Auden. Before his death, Auden acknowledged his authorship of an explicitly erotic poem, "The Platonic Blow" by "Miss Oral." "The Platonic Blow" is an illustration of how rhyme and meter can function to create a distance between the reader and the erotic experience which occasioned the poem. In thirty-five smooth quatrains, Auden's narrator tells the story of his encounter with a twenty-four-year-old mechanic named Bud. Attracted to the young man by the sight of his forceful torso in white T-shirt and blue denims, the narrator invites him up to his room and performs fellatio on him. The poem is a graceful, celebratory rendering of sexual experience. The easy rhythm of the lines is almost hypnotizing, making it possible for the reader to respond sympathetically to a rather graphic description of anilingus. Poetic form depersonalizes the erotic experience, just as laughter does.

"The Platonic Blow" appeared in an underground literary magazine of the sixties called *Fuck You/A Magazine of the Arts*. *Fuck You* was the only literary magazine in the world devoted primarily to the publication of erotic poetry. It was certainly the only journal of the time where "The Platonic Blow" could be printed. Its editor, the poet Ed

Sanders (*Peace Eye*), was in the position of editing the only publication in America where American poets like Allen Ginsberg, Harry Fainlight, Al Fowler, Lenore Kandel, Joel Oppenheimer, Carol Bergé, Gene Bloom, Eric Weinberger, Robert Creeley, John Wieners, Diane di Prima, Paul Blackburn, and Michael McClure—many important names in the Beat and post-Beat generation of poets—could publish their occasional erotic poems.

Their major accomplishment was to close the distance between erotic experience and its presentation by writing directly and graphically about sexuality. A few of them, particularly Sanders, wrote humorous erotic poems, but generally speaking they achieved a tone of intimate sincerity by avoiding humor and conventional poetic form.

The subjects of their poems often seem drawn from personal experience. The elegant lyric poet John Wieners writes graphically about homosexual encounters without ever seeming vulgar—because the moment of passion is expressed in equally passionate words that invite comparison with similar moments in Catullus' lyrics. Like Wieners, Clive Matson is able in his first book, *Mainline to the Heart* (1966) to write with graceful explicitness of physical love as he chronicles the breakup of his marriage. In Wieners, Matson, and a number of other poets, a passionate sincerity restores to four-letter words their original purity. Poets are the keepers of the language, and for the poets of the sixties this applied to the Anglo-Saxon vocabulary of sexuality. In their poems words like "cock," "cunt" and "fuck" are stripped of their pejorative connotations, and seem freshly viable when properly used to describe sexual experience. Far from writing obscene poems, these poets reclaimed useful words for use in their proper context.

Although most of the poets whose work appeared in *Fuck You/A Magazine of the Arts* wrote erotic poetry about specific situations—imagined or otherwise—Michael McClure in his "Fuck Ode" uses the Anglo-Saxon words to beautiful effect in celebrating eroticism in the abstract. His ecstatic vision of huge figures making love recalls the emotional climax achieved by Blake in his visionary poems. Ed Sanders mixes ancient Egyptian lore with original verbal constructions ("piss-quakes," "squack" "toe-queens") to create erotic poems in which language disorientation and humor give a mythical significance to sexuality.

Harry Fainlight and Al Fowler are two of the few poets of the sixties whose reputation is based almost entirely on their erotic poetry. Fainlight pays attention to the tradition of English poetry without distancing himself from his experience. Fowler, like Joel Oppenheimer, Carol Bergé, Paul Blackburn, Eric Weinberger and Sam Abrams (author of *Barbara*) writes erotic poems about specific situations that demonstrate how the influence of Pound, Williams, and Charles Olson was carried over intact from "straight" poetry to their erotic verse. These poems are marked by plain speech, detailed observation, and abrupt endings which often resemble the punch line of a joke. The reader is presented with a block of experience and then left dangling at the end, a method which allows for a maximum impact that is almost orgasmic in nature.

This is illustrated by a poem of Al Fowler's entitled "Musée Des Beaux Enfants" in which he imagines himself a Sunday school teacher taking children to a museum full of objects which might be used sexually; the word "fuck" used only once and falling at the end of the poem creates ripples which run back through the poem. An even better illustration might be Joel Oppenheimer's "Poem In Praise Of Perseverance," in which he describes the frustration between lovers in sexual terms, and ends the poem with a reference to "popular tunes"—which serves to emphasize the repetitiousness of a long love affair.

What is unique in these erotic poems is an unembarrassed acceptance of sexuality and obscenity. Humorous or conventionally formalistic poets distance themselves from their subject matter, but the straightforward approach of the new erotic poets demonstrates that there need be nothing embarrassing about the serious exploration of erotic experience.

Just as recent erotic fiction has had a liberating effect on the treatment of sex in general fiction, so have the poems published in *Fuck You/A Magazine of the Arts* had a liberating effect on contemporary poetry. Certainly women poets like Anne Waldman and Diane Wakoski—to name only two of many—write more openly about sexual experience because of the example set by those poems.

Yet it must be confessed that—with the sole exception of Lenore Kandel, author of *The Love Book* (1965) and *Word Alchemy* (1967)—there are at present no poets who publish mainly erotic poetry.

While it is true that a number of well known poets, among them Erica Jong, Anne Sexton, and Marilyn Hacker (whose collection, *Presentation Piece* includes some superb erotic poems written in traditional verse forms), have written erotic poetry, none of them is regarded as a strictly erotic poet.

Kandel's work is not exclusively erotic, but the major part of it is. Her erotic poems, she has said, deal with the evocation of the divinity in man through the medium of physical love. Her writing is straightforward in its descriptions of various sexual acts, and yet she manages to imbue them with a celebratory tone by returning to the theme of transcendence through eroticism. She states as much in her preface to *World Alchemy*.

> Two poems of mine, published as a small book, deal with physical love and the invocation, recognition, and acceptance of the divinity in man through the medium of physical love. In other words, it feels good. It feels so good

that you can step outside your private ego and share the grace of the universe. . . .

Unfortunately, Kandel is not a particularly inventive poet, and her reliance on clichés like "big grand and terrible" to describe the penis in a poem entitled "To Fuck With Love" serves to dilute the honest force of her sexual invocations of human divinity. Like McClure in his "Fuck Ode," Kandel attempts to recreate the ecstatic moment when "you can step outside your private ego and share the grace of the universe." Her method, like McClure's, is to imitate the rhythm of sexual intercourse by a calculated use of specifically sexual imagery, repetition of certain key phrases, a liberal use of exclamation marks, and an orgasmic emphasis on eroticism as a means of sharing "the grace of the universe." Unfortunately contemporary poetry does not reflect the possibilities inherent in the encounter between the poet and eros. The reasons for this are understandable, but as Kandel points out, "When a poet censors his vision, he no longer tells the truth as he sees it."

IX

THE WOMAN'S ROLE: NOVELIST AND VICTIM

ONE OF THE MOST telling arguments against erotic literature is that its treatment of female characters is distorted by male fantasy. Up until the fifties erotic literature was written solely by men; critics have argued persuasively that the male writer depicted women as fantasy figures or objects of sexual abuse, but never as people. Because of such distortions, critics like Steven Marcus have indicted erotic literature for its lack of reality. Victorian erotica, Marcus showed, is particularly vulnerable to attack along these lines, but there is ample evidence that until recently the genre as a whole has been guilty as charged. Male erotic novelists drew their female characters from adolescent fantasies, depicting women as prostitutes, nymphomaniacs, Thurberesque monsters, creatures of mystery; objects for degradation and physical abuse at the hands of male characters. In erotic fiction women were willing and submissive, puppet-like—or they were raped.

No valid literature can be based on the abuse of half the human race, which is perhaps why people with only a superficial knowledge of erotic literature—based on readings of the worst examples of the genre—have been so quick to dismiss it. One of the objectives of this book, however, is to acquaint these people with the masterpieces of the genre, books by both male and female writers which do not abuse women. Admittedly, the run of the mill erotic novel most people are likely to see is usually guilty of distorting female sexuality, but this is not true of French erotic literature nor of the best American erotic literature of the past ten years. (However, it may come as a surprise to many that when women began writing erotic novels their depiction of female characters confirmed in a number of ways the insights of male novelists. *Story of O* is a perfect example of this, as are many of the novels by women discussed in this chapter.)

But before we begin to examine the role of women—as both writers and characters—in erotic literature, some reference point is needed for purposes of comparison. Robert Moore's *Lady Killer* (1969) is perhaps an extreme example of how women are degraded in genre novels, but that only makes it a more startling illustration of the abusive tendencies in erotic fiction.

Moore's protagonist, Jim Butler, is a Mafia contract killer whose specialty is murdering women, in various gruesome ways, after raping them. The considerable power of the novel—it is both frightening and repulsive—is the result of two factors: the author's ability to create a suspenseful story so that you read on against your will, fascinated by the horrors he so coolly unfolds; and the lack of any moral vision.

Moore is a competent writer who writes of women in *Lady Killer* and *The Rape Conspiracy* (1971) with the cold, dispassionate eye of a scientist describing the process of vivisection. The horrible acts of violence committed by the killer are described with amoral relish, and the author obviously intends them to titillate the destructive impulse in us, just as he intends his descriptions of rape to stimulate us sexually. This is pathology rather than literature, of course, because unlike Sade or Réage, Moore is not describing horror to make a point—even that there is none—and for that reason *Lady Killer* reads like the fictional equivalent of a case history in *Psychopathia Sexualis*.

Moore's spare, hard-boiled prose strikes a chord of response somewhere in us, however. Despite its lack of vision, *Lady Killer* reminds us of the negative Dionysian impulse to destruction.

Moore's treatment of his women characters through all the fiendishly detailed descriptions of murder in *Lady Killer* is so repugnant that it may obscure more subtle crimes against them. To begin with, we have the woman as victim. Trapped, at the mercy of the killer's superior force, women submit to degradation in the hope of being spared.

> His heart was pounding like a triphammer, and he heard the girl's breathing next to his ear, fast and shallow, and interspersed with cries of pain. He was certain she felt no pleasure from the act, not even an unwelcome physical pleasure. It was an act of agony and humiliation to her, just as it was one of ecstasy and exultation to him. . . .

Throughout the novel, Moore's protagonist can only achieve full potency when he is about to rape, "to force his will on a woman who was horror struck at what was about to happen." It is only necessary to add that the other side of this treatment of women as unwilling sexual victims is the even more popular treatment of them as sexually insatiable.

Naturally when women are victimized in this kind of

erotic novel, they are also presented as stupid, helpless, or promiscuous. The image of the all-powerful male inflicting rape and death at will is seldom countered by a powerful female image. Then there is the explicit male distrust of and contempt for women, based on his fear and hatred of the sex. These are the important characteristics of the abusive treatment of women characters in some erotic fiction.

Bearing in mind this description of abusive erotic fiction by male writers, look now at how women writers treat their female characters when they write erotic novels. We have discussed in earlier chapters the work of Pauline Réage, Harriet Daimler, and a few other women, but from a different perspective. They were simply erotic novelists, regardless of their sex. But considering how badly women have fared in conventional novels of the genre, this perspective can be limiting. A more fruitful approach will be to compare how male writers see women in novels like *Lady Killer,* and in better books, with how women see themselves—and men—in their erotic novels. Where the two views converge and where they diverge should tell us a great deal about erotic literature in general, and help to place women erotic writers in perspective.

Women novelists, in general, can claim no more sensitivity or insightfulness in their treatment of female characters than men. There are differences, but they are mostly of degree. It might be said that women are a trifle more romantic about sexuality, for instance, but not always. It certainly isn't true of Lela Seftali's *Ride a Cock-Horse* (1970), the most remarkable novel by a member of either sex published by Olympia Press in New York.

Ride a Cock-Horse contains more attention to sensuous detail than is found in erotic fiction by males. Seftali lingers over descriptions of non-sexual physical details, building an atmosphere around her first-person narrator that is almost tangible, offering it to the reader in place of plot and characterization. It is *poetic* in the best sense of the poetic evocation of sensuous detail. It is also extremely subjective and almost narcissistic in its total concentration on one woman, the narrator. All that we learn about her arises naturally from her actions and reflections: she lives alone, she doesn't worry about money, she uses a lot of drugs, and she refers often—with some bitterness—to her parents. Above all, she is isolated. Her narration consists of a string of sexual episodes, which generally follow the same pattern. She arouses herself with drugs in her apartment, and then she ventures out into the streets to find someone to share a wide variety of erotic tastes with. Independent, isolated by choice, she needs other people only for sex.

Unlike the women in erotic fiction by men, she is aware of her role in male fantasies.

> I am fantasy. I am masturbation. I am a receptacle for all the male orgasms of the world. . . . Men would like to masturbate on me, defile me, denigrate me, or put me on the pedestal. . . . I am a groaning smorgasboard for everyone, a banquet table. It is difficult to reconcile myself to who I am.

Like Genet, she evokes a sensual atmosphere conducive to masturbation, but unlike him she is graphically explicit in her descriptions of erotic activity. Her romanticism is intellectual, and it doesn't soften the physical details of sex. She says, "My strength is my sexuality. . . . I preserve my own desire at all costs."

What must be stressed is her self-containment. "I live from myself, and, therefore, I live for myself." Elsewhere, she says, "I want to say, 'I am your personal verb. I am unrelated in time to anyone else like a flapping window shade, out of context.' "

Her sole connections with other people are made when she leaves her apartment in search of sex. She encounters a black rapist, a Hell's Angels motorcyclist, an old Italian bachelor, a group of tourists—all lovers *she* chooses, uses solely for sex, and then leaves. Her desire is the life force that guides her and connects her to other people, and yet she does not despair, does not feel cheated of anything.

Ride a Cock-Horse, like *Our Lady of the Flowers,* is a mirror held up to both the protagonist and the reader for the purpose of masturbation. It is all surface: the narrator knows that other people use her as their "personal verb," and that she can adapt herself to any of their fantasies while never surrendering herself except during sex. She is always aware that "the cunt can feel, that the cunt is intelligent, that the penis can think."

Seftali has written one of the few recent erotic novels that can bear comparison with the masterpieces of Genet or Réage; she writes with sensitivity, intelligence, and honesty, and in *Ride a Cock-Horse* she has shown that women's erotic writing resists categorization. She is by turns intensely subjective and romantic, then objectively, even harshly realistic in sex passages; she creates an atmosphere of sensuous mystery in which her protagonist is able to be strong, independent, and practical. Her self-containment suggests that one of the important characteristics of erotic fiction by women is the depiction of strong, independent women. In erotic fiction by men, male characters are seldom self-contained; they must affect other characters in order to realize their own natures. Female characters are usually dependent upon men, or seen in intimate conjunction with men.

There is also a tendency to inject female sexual fantasies into erotic fiction by women—as if to say to male writers, we've read your fantasies about us, now we'll create our own. *The Party* (1971) written by Uta West under the pseudonym Renee Auden, is an example of how specifically female fantasies may be incorporated into a realistic narrative that—without the fantasies—might have been written by a man. The protagonist of *The Party* is a wealthy rock star groupie named Felicity whose emotional life consists of the sexual fantasies she has during concerts by singers like Mick Jagger, Jim Morrison, and Jimi Hendrix. When she has a bad experience with LSD during Jagger's Altamont concert, she goes home to England and her family. She thinks of her stay with a mother who hates her as a rest cure, until she begins having an affair with her younger brother, and her mother forces her to leave. Desperate after another bad experience during a rock concert fantasy, she sees a Freudian analyst in the hope that he can assist her in making the transition from a lifestyle that doesn't work to something better. A singer named Bruce attracts her, perhaps because he shares her preoccupation with fantasy. Eventually, after she leaves her therapist and takes part with Bruce in the acting out of both their fantasies, she achieves a certain happiness.

The point Auden makes is that, for Felicity, fantasy life is not enough. Even though her fantasies are satisfying in many respects—they are specifically female, and she is often in command of the situation—a life of drugs, sex, and fantasy is not enough to sustain her. Unlike the narrator of *Ride a Cock-Horse,* she is not self-contained, and she finds fulfillment only within a relationship with a man. *The Party* is a successful treatment of the theme of fantasy versus reality, but Auden's *High Thrust,* a futuristic satire about an organization called The Management which arranges people's sex lives and offers them robots as sex partners, is not nearly as good.

Pure fantasy (as opposed to sexual fantasies in a realistic context) is an important vehicle for a number of female erotic novelists, particularly Deneen Peckinpah and Merril Harris. Peckinpah's *Ceremonies of Love* (1970) is perhaps the most experimental erotic novel to appear since the work of the French surrealists—indeed, Peckinpah's method of telling a story of a young woman's symbolic progress through her own consciousness is reminiscent at times of Lautréamont and Rimbaud.

> The body in which she will move through this story, through this journey, will be the exposed body of the inner woman. You who read this adventure may find that body quite strange, but it is real and it is her own. Fantasy, dream, waking life . . . all are weathers of the same reality. . . .
> Writing as bleeding. Occasional spotting, until the words begin to flow, at last, down the insides of my legs. . . . My story's lunatic.

Thus Peckinpah describes her method. Her protagonist sets off on a journey toward a state of being, which is described by her mysterious guide, Andro Jean, as the place where unity is attained through eroticism. "As I said, there's no duality in the realm where I dwell. When you made love you completed yourselves. . . ."

Supposedly the narrator is journeying through Africa, but her travel is internal. She meets fabulous beasts and makes love to a man whose leg is a penis. To get somewhere, all she has to do is stick her head in a lion's mouth. She is constantly aware of her fragmented state of being. "(Sex is) . . . the only thing that makes my fucking multiplicity bearable. I realize exactly how fragmented I am. . . ."

At times she despairs, particularly after making love with a spider:

> God, like a cruel father, has thrown us into the middle of a boundless ocean. To what end? Ah, mystery, indeed. And all of us trying to swim for shore! What a laugh!

In the end the narrator returns to the "normal" world, having discovered the secret of womanhood in her journey through herself. *Ceremonies of Love* is a difficult, often self-indulgent book that uses fantasy as a vehicle to enter one woman's consciousness. The end dovetails with the beginning, a circular movement also found in Merril Harris' fantasy take off on *Alice in Wonderland, Dirty Alice* (1970).

Dirty Alice resembles *Ceremonies of Love* in the sense that it also describes a fantastic journey. But Harris' third-person narration of a modern, sexual Alice's cavortings with rabbits and Lilliputians is a conventional retelling of Lewis Carroll's story, and she doesn't succeed in creating the subjective, intimate atmosphere of *Ceremonies of Love*. The story begins with scenes showing Alice as a child being sexually and physically abused by a mad father. She is removed from the situation by a bestial figure who invites her to come dance with him, and from that encounter she enters a world as strange as the original Alice's, but nowhere near as enchanting.

A female fantasist who writes under the name of Salambo Forest was the most prolific author of pure fantasies published by Olympia Press. Two of her most characteristically romantic novels are *Witch Power* and *Fire Child*. Witchcraft, astrology, and magic are prominent features of her fiction, which is flawed by trite thinking and a clichéd writing style resembling at times the excesses of true confession magazines. Forest's kind of syrupy fantasy for women is probably the closest female equivalent to the male fantasies in the genre.

One woman writer, Mary Sativa, author of the very contemporary *Acid Temple Ball* discussed earlier, extended the range of fantasy by incorporating elements of it into an historical novel called *The Lovers' Crusade* (1971). In the middle of the fourteenth century, a monk named Father Andreas is returning with the Christian armies from Byzantium to Cologne. He carries with him an ancient manuscript describing pagan rites, and is accompanied on his journey by a Moslem scholar who will help interpret the manuscript. Along the way he encounters a gallery of medieval characters whose lives are briefly sketched along the conventional lines of historical romance. The fantasy element in these scenes makes them seem dream-like, although Sativa's many erotic sequences are as realistic as any in *Acid Temple Ball*. Sativa's two novels are vastly different in language, structure, and setting, but romanticism is at the heart of both. Compare these lines from *The Lovers' Crusade* with the second passage, taken from *Acid Temple Ball.*

The blind minstrel pulled her close to him, soothing her. "Tell me what is in here. See for me, Eleanor," Forest begged.

"The windows are as bright as dreams," she murmured against his chest.

"Tell me, describe them to me, Eleanor."

"Red and gold and blue—angels, saints, their faces are white and peaceful . . . they smile. And there is a naked man and woman, her belly is round and high, and they stand in a field of blood-red roses."

. . . Unbearable desire to see him, and break the walls of daily reality. His smile and my scornful misery cannot exist in the same universe; I could forget him, but once he touches me again, mystery and joy will flood this winter city, necessity will crumble before chance and change. I am eager and afraid. . . .

Unrelated passages, yet they share a romantic tone, they suggest that Sativa draws deeply from the well of fantasy to "break the walls of daily reality."

Of course it is possible to be a romantic writer without incorporating personal fantasies into a story, just as there is a difference between personal fantasies and fantasies which have universal appeal because they originate in the literary imagination. Abusive novels like *Lady Killer* usually originate in personal fantasies, and so do some of the novels by women discussed here. In such novels, from Victorian erotica to *Salambo Forest*, characters do not exist independent of the author's limited personal designs for them. They are puppets whose function is to act out these fantasies to the satisfaction of the author. This kind of fantasy is not structured by the demands of art, nor is it transformed into fiction of universal applicability. In a sense all art originates in fantasy, but the fantasy material does not become art until it ceases to be personal. The strong current of fantasy evident in erotic fiction by women takes a realistic form less often than in novels by men; yet although women seem more comfortable with pure fantasy than men, they are capable of writing strongly realistic novels.

Jane Gallion's two novels, *Biker* (1969) and *Stoned* (1969), are brutally realistic, and only one, *Biker*, might be called romantic. It is also the most violent. Gallion sets her novel in the future, after a revolution has returned the American West to primitive savagery, a barren ghostland full of marauding motorcycle gangs.

The protagonist is a young woman who has been so brutalized by these predatory Neanderthals that she has become an animal herself. The opening scene shows her being raped repeatedly, desperately trying to hang onto some part of her identity. She kills one of her attackers and escapes on her own motorcycle, sustained by amphetamine and fear. To her all men are pack animals who want to abuse her, and she takes her revenge when she can.

> They are still asleep, the pigs, and so satisfied, dreaming their private dreams in the wallows of their minds, and she knows that she is no more than a dream chick, who moves and talks and fucks and loves in the halls and passageways of his head, and what he wants from her and she wants to give is only another shuck. . . . She stops, standing over him, looking down at his sleeping face, and she will not pity him for being as trapped as she. Someone has to suffer, someone has to hurt and bleed because there is nothing else to feel but pain. . . . She hits him hard with the rock and he makes no sound. . . .

This scene is the result of her disillusionment with a man she encounters in the ruins of Las Vegas who persuades her that he's different from the other bikers—so that instead of victimizing her as she expects, he wants her to want him. Their relationship grows, she begins to regain her trust of other people, and then he betrays her by offering her sexual services to another biker in return for drugs.

Gallion creates a nightmare world in vivid language, shifting to a stream of consciousness technique to describe her protagonist's feelings every time she is brutalized. Gallion's romanticism is dark and frightening, but it is apparent in her character's disillusionment with love—which she concludes is a "shuck" by the end of the novel. Her disillusionment is exacerbated by an encounter with a self-proclaimed messiah named Chris, who runs his own commune on the idea of a love she cannot believe in. Possibly part of the reason she feels that love, too, is illusory are statements like this from the relatively enlightened Chris.

> "You think broads have to have kids to know where it's at?"
>
> "Of course," he stated positively. "That's why they have wombs. They have breasts to feed kids. The body you are in determines how you must relate to the world. Men have penises so they can fertilize women. It's all preset by the physical envelope in which you find yourself."

Yet still the "love shuck" is necessary, because Gallion's protagonist has seen the alternative.

> She decided to make Chris sweat for not having to face the truth like she had, the awful truth that made the love shuck so necessary. He'd never found out that the lie was the only truth there was. . . .

Biker is futuristic and violent, like many Essex House novels; *Stoned* is a different kind of book altogether, indicating Gallion's wide range, and her preoccupation with desperate women. The protagonist of *Stoned* is trapped like the heroine of *Biker,* but her circumstances are more familiar. Elaine Stuart is a lower-middle-class housewife with two children and a husband as frustrated as she is. She complains that he won't make love to her as often as she wants, and he responds with his own complaints about her nagging and the economic circumstances which trap him. Gallion is superb at depicting this kind of soap opera milieu. She has an ear that takes note of babies crying, and household duties performed before the television set. She describes the lives of millions of frustrated housewives without a trace of romanticism, but with enough objectivity to make Elaine's husband Randy a sympathetic figure. Everyone in *Stoned* is trapped by the small details of lower-middle-class life.

> By the time her calculations told her that the top seventeen layers of dirt would be soaked off them, she had put the last pan in the dish drainer and was wiping the sodden bits of Crappen Crunch off the table with the dish sponge. She tossed the sponge in the sink and sat down, hoping for a minute's peace. But the bathroom door burst open, delivering the dripping children who were grinning satanically and slopping water in all directions. She got up and found towels for them, thinking with grim determination that she had the rest of the day to clean up the various messes and knowing that she would need nearly every minute. . . .

Elaine finds her escape in marijuana, which is given to her for the first time by a friend who sees that she's at her wit's end. The drug causes a sexual revolution in Elaine and Randy's life. Sexually satisfied, marijuana available to spirit her away from her role as frustrated housewife, Elaine is better able to endure her constricted life. With detailed realism, Gallion rubs the reader's face in dirty diapers, screaming children, and marital arguments, doing for the lower-middle-class housewife what Hubert Selby, Jr. does for his lower-class characters in *Last Exit to Brooklyn*. At one point, she has Elaine say,

> "I do know that I can't go on playing this picket fence and fat babies game I've been playing without losing what's left of my mind in the process. . . .

In this world, sex is necessary but illusionary, like love itself. As in *Biker,* everything is a "shuck." Sex and drugs offer only temporary escape from the trap that Gallion sees as the condition of life for her women characters.

Our attempt to discover the distinguishing marks of erotic fiction written by women reveals as many contradictory elements in the work of Jane Gallion as it does in the work of Harriet Daimler, Deneen Peckinpah, Mary Sativa, Renee Auden, and Lela Seftali. But her women characters, like theirs, are survivors. Their characters are tough-minded, independent people even when they decide to play a submissive sexual role, as Louise Walbrook's character Louise does, in the story of a strong woman's fascination with an even stronger man, *Gordon* (1966).

The novel opens with Louise sitting in a London pub on a sunny day shortly after the end of the Second World War. As she sits there she thinks with contempt of the weak men who have attempted to seduce her. Then her wrist is taken in strong fingers and she is drawn into the street by a man whose simple approach—it continues through the novel —is to treat her like a child. He invites her home to see his garden, and there he seduces her before she has time to react. She is resentful, but nevertheless attracted to the strange man, whom she later learns is a psychiatrist. She responds to something dark and primitive in his treatment of her with a childish fascination. ". . . he must have guessed in me the same willingness to go under, to play Gretchen to his Mephisto-driven Faust."

Despite the fact that he never once, in the course of their affair, treats her with affection, she doesn't resist his cruel treatment of her. Not that he is the familiar sadist of English erotica; his cruelty is emotional. He enjoys being rough with her in their lovemaking, but no matter how hard he pushes her, he can't find her limits. After he has been a particularly brutal lover, she thinks:

> But with my indignation there flowed a satisfaction, like the mingling of wine with water, that he had not only held

me in his power and inflicted pain on me, but had left the painful traces of possessing me on my body. "I wish I could have been deflowered by him," I thought, "instead of that fool ox of a man at that time."

Dr. Richard Gordon is her lover's name, and Walbrook puts his professional role to ironic use. The author does not cheat her theme by making her protagonist stupid, or unintelligent. The key perhaps is that with Gordon Louise feels secure, as in a father-daughter relationship; but more than that, she is attracted by the knowledge that he cares enough about her to break through all her unsatisfactory, modern defenses.

> When he possessed me so fiercely that he drove me to the brink of darkness he gave me the ecstasy of knowing that I had reached the one thing, the only thing I had ever wanted.
> When he was about to take me, I was yearning for him to shatter me and to break me down, and perhaps that was the reason why I mostly made difficulties. . . .

When Gordon disappears from her life, Louise doesn't find out until years later—from a psychiatrist friend of Gordon's—that her lover was frightened of her encouragement of his excesses, that she drove him to dark places in himself that led to his suicide. The novel ends with chilling impact, when Louise falls in love with Gordon's psychiatrist friend, who also finds himself seduced by Louise's limitless submissiveness. The point here, I believe, is not Louise's weakness, for she is not weak; she is drawn as a strong, intelligent woman, like O. Because of her strength, she is able to manipulate Gordon to achieve her goal—which is to have her individual ego mastered by someone worthy of becoming one with, someone who cares enough about her to take the awful risks involved in assuming total emotional responsibility for her.

This is the kind of relationship sought by the female protagonist of a beautiful short novel called either *Sicily*

Enough (when it first appeared in *Olympia Review,* the magazine of The Olympia Press, under the name Claire Rabe) or *Flesh and Blood* (1962) when it was published in a book with another short novel under the name of Anna Winter. *Sicily Enough* is the story of an American woman, the mother of three children, who, when the novel opens, has just arrived in a small town in Sicily.

The woman is seduced by the animal sexuality of Sicily and Sicilians, and the author evokes this atmosphere in prose which sensuously describes the sights, smells, and feel of the hot, primitive island.

> Every woman has breasts and thighs and hair in her armpits; I see them as black curling flowers. Their legs are strong and hairy, men do not force them to shave; here they do not alter animals or their passions.
> This directness, this use of the body attracts me at once to the Sicilians and makes me feel warm. There is no subtle sex here, no American sex, but coupling itself. . . .

Winter's protagonist feels herself swimming in the warm ocean of primitive sexuality. She has an affair with a man from the village who makes love to her as if they are both beasts, without the slightest regard for her personal identity.

> We make love like religion. He lets out my name with his sperm and I feel adored in a way that no virgin has ever been prayed to. . . .

Yet in the end, she is disillusioned by her lover's male stupidity, and realizes that the affair was only a way of forgetting, for a brief time, her own undefined *malaise.*

I have said that the one feature shared by all the women novelists discussed in this chapter is the creation of strong female characters. A less important characteristic, shared by only some of the writers discussed here, is a use of different modes of fantasy, employed to create a more subjective, intimate fictional world than is found in erotic writing by men.

Beyond this, it is only possible to suggest, with some hesitancy, that many of the best women writing erotic novels have chosen as their theme the most important in the genre: eroticism as a means of transcending the painful, individual ego. Like the authors of homosexual erotic fiction—and indeed, like many of the finest erotic novelists—they often choose to express this theme within a sadomasochistic context; but whether it is merely implied or heavily emphasized, we must remember that what is important is not the rituals and paraphernalia of sadomasochism, but the goal of transcendence.

X

HOMOSEXUAL
EROTIC FICTION

> Joy is marvelous! That's what these
> books have, I guess . . . a joy of the
> flesh. And I can't help but feel that
> they do more psychological good for
> more people than all of the hun-
> dreds of textbook tracts and treatises
> about love-ways between men.
> —ANGELO D'ARCANGELO, writing
> of Richard Amory's *Song of
> the Loon* series

WE MAY ACCOUNT for the relatively small number of erotic
novels that deal with homosexuality by remembering that
instead of receiving its proper recognition as another form
of human love, homosexuality has always headed society's
list of perversions. Thus when we discuss homosexual erotic
fiction we must suspend any preconceived notions about

sexual categories if we are to arrive at an understanding of the work.

That there are so few good homosexual erotic novels is not because of a dearth of good writers who also happen to be homosexual—one thinks of E. M. Forster not allowing *Maurice* (1972), to be published until after his death—but because of the stigma society has always attached to love between members of the same sex. The career of Oscar Wilde is probably the most famous instance of the sanctions that may be brought against homosexual writers. (No wonder Wilde would not acknowledge authorship of one of the most interesting homosexual erotic novels, *Teleny or The Reverse of the Medal* (1893). The case of Jean Cocteau is no different. Most critics believe that he wrote *The White Paper* (1956)—a man's confession of his love for boys—but he would sign his name only to the preface of the book, where he evades the question.

> *The White Paper*, whence does it come, who wrote it? Did I? Perhaps. Another? Probably. Are we not become others the moment after we've done writing? . . . . Would *The White Paper* be autobiographical then? Then I refuse its paternity, for what I find charming here is that the author talks without talking himself.

The list of homosexual artists in history is not as lengthy as some homosexuals claim, but it does include many excellent writers who might have contributed to homosexual erotic literature. Many writers who are homosexual may have wanted to write erotic novels, but had they done so they were likely to get into more trouble than heterosexual authors of erotic novels. Those few brave enough to write their erotic novels, wrote in the closet, in the dark; naturally their approach was heavily influenced by their awareness of society's disapproval.

With only a few exceptions, the homosexual erotic novel cannot be said to have much of a history before the sixties.

Among these exceptions are *The Young and Evil* (1933) by the poets Charles Henri Ford and Parker Tyler, and *The Gaudy Image* (1958) by William Talsman. (Jean Genet is the most notable homosexual erotic writer of this period, but his work is discussed in a previous chapter.)

The Young and Evil is more remarkable for the experimental nature of its prose than for its discreet treatment of homosexual eroticism, but the authors employ a narrative tone that is expressive of homosexual themes without being sexually explicit. Obviously influenced by the prose repetitions of Gertrude Stein, *The Young and Evil* owes almost as large a debt to Djuna Barnes. The authors went to Stein for their run-on sentences and repetitive prose, but the world created by this technique is Barnesian—and bleak.

The novel opens with a surrealistic nursery tale about the homosexuality of a young poet named Karel:

> Well said the wolf to Little Red Riding Hood no sooner was Karel seated in the Round table than the impossible happened. There before him stood a fairy prince and one of those mythological creatures known as Lesbians. . . .

The story, such as it is, revolves about Karel and his friends and lovers, among whom is Julian. Karel meets Julian at the dock in New York just after Julian arrives from New Orleans.

> He knew that this was Karel. For one thing he expected eyelashes made up with mascara. . . .
> Karel was like a tall curved building only much smaller. He was wearing a dark green, the color of the rings around the holes, hat with an upward sweep on the left side. His overcoat seemed to fit him desperately.

Although *The Young and Evil* is perhaps most memorable for its depiction of the homosexual literary subculture in the New York of the early thirties, it is also about the difficulty of maintaining a homosexual relationship. Besides

Karel and Julian, there are three other major characters in
the novel, Louis, a woman named Theodosia, and Gabriel.
Both Julian and Gabriel attempt to form heterosexual relationships with Theodosia but fail, just as in the end Karel's
homosexual relationship with Louis fails—and the novel
ends with Karel screaming as Louis jealously attacks him.
Probably the most direct statement of the novel's theme
occurs in a scene when Karel has just left Julian. Julian
decides that love relationships between people are impossible to sustain.

> He doubted the sincerity of the people he saw living
> together supposedly in love. He had never known physical
> and mental love towards a single person. It had always been
> completely one or the other. With Karel it was the other.
> With Louis really neither. He was unbelieving when he saw
> lovers who were lovers in the complete sense and who slept
> night after night in the same bed. He was quite sure their
> love was a fabrication or a convenience or a recompense and
> he did not believe in their love as love.

The action of the book consists of bitchy squabbles and
frustrated love affairs; nothing of great moment happens
during the course of the narrative, but the language creates
a hot-house atmosphere, a brittle, elegant surface beneath
which lies a frightening vacancy.

The Gaudy Image shows the influence of Jean Genet
on almost every page. It is, in fact, the application of Genet's
special vision to America. Talsman's characters, like Genet's,
are petty hoodlums, and like Genet, Talsman transforms
these tough-talking, brutal characters through the casual elegance of his language.

The Gaudy Image begins on an elegiacal note with a
portrait of a delicate "lady" named Titania (Tit for short),
but then in the following chapter it dips into the underworld when Titania visits a pool hall hoping to pick someone up. Titania is Talsman's equivalent of the figure of

Divine in *Our Lady of the Flowers*. She unites the narrative by her presence in most of the novel's important scenes. The relationship of an older ex-convict named Gunner with a reformatory school graduate named Nickie Machete is typical of the brutal relationships between men in the book. Nickie looks up to Gunner, but Gunner is cruel and boastful with him, making the boy an accomplice in his crimes. Other characters have fanciful names reminiscent of Genet: Passion Flower, Hot Hole, Pelvis, and Bengal. These people come together briefly, then bounce away from each other, in a seedy world of bars, furnished rooms, and pool halls, always looking for the next pick-up and the next sexual encounter. The mixture of elegant language and gutter slang makes for a gaudy surface, like a metropolitan street which, when seen from afar, still retains in its buildings the outlines of a prouder past, but up close is all neon and decay. It is perfect for depicting the kind of homosexual underworld where toughness and flights of ornate rhetoric coexist.

With the exception of *The Young and Evil* and *The Gaudy Image,* novels expressing homosexual eroticism were no bolder than novels about heterosexual love until the early sixties. The necessity for discretion neutered novels like *Finisterre* and *The City and the Pillar,* and yet when they were published these books were considered daring treatments of a forbidden theme. In a chapter of *The Homosexual Handbook* (1969) devoted to homosexual books, the author, Angelo d'Arcangelo (Joseph Bush), lists most of these blushing bestsellers; few writers chronicle the gay world with more authority—and none so amusingly—as d'Arcangelo. Here is his description of the Gay Novel.

> The Gay Novel has a certain tradition. It's grown into a kind of art form and has its own style, formula and rationale. Due to a widening permissiveness on the part of the law, and a greater willingness of publishing houses to take advantage of it, a very wide audience for this sort of material is devour-

ing great amounts of homosexual fiction. But this is rather a new thing. When I was young the classic Gay Novel was passed around like the Eucharist, with moist eyes and a warm endorsement. . . .

D'Arcangelo's description of *Finisterre* as "the subliminal measure of what a Gay Novel should be" is followed by an analysis of it which applies to most of the gay novels that followed.

The book tastefully avoided any graphic description of the sexual activities of the lovers; they might as well have only indulged in handholding and an occasional French kiss on high holidays. The whole business reeked of doom. . . .

D'Arcangelo goes on to describe similar books with homosexual themes or characters, but he has made an important point about the classic Gay Novel: discretion and a consciousness of doom—punishment for inversion—characterize these timid books.

According to d'Arcangelo, homosexual readers turned to mainstream fiction like *Giovanni's Room* by James Baldwin, *Eustace Chisholm and the Works* by James Purdy, *A Single Man* by Christopher Isherwood, Mary Renault's historical novels about ancient Greece, *Myra Breckinridge* by Gore Vidal, and *City of Night* and *Numbers* by John Rechy. Rechy's two novels are notable for their depiction of the world of the male prostitute in a style that combines toughness with an awkward poetry.

It is difficult to improve on d'Arcangelo's list of novels that have appealed to gay readers in the past twenty-five years until we look at his own books, which along with Richard Amory's *Song of the Loon* mark the beginning of a freer homosexual erotic literature. But before continuing with Amory and "Uncle Fudge" (as d'Arcangelo styles himself in *The Homosexual Handbook*), we should look more closely at the strong tendency in homosexual erotic writing to follow Genet's lead in viewing the gay world from the gutter up. A two-volume novel by Philip Barrows called *Whores, Queers and Others*, published in 1967 by The Olympia Press, reflects the same fascination with the sordid underworld of homosexual pick-ups and casual sex with prostitutes as Talsman's *The Gaudy Image* or Rechy's two novels. It is a dispassionate record of a man's sexual life—an ex-seminarian haunted by the idea of a punishing God—as he moves from sexual encounter to sexual encounter across America and Europe. The writing is literate and low-keyed, the sex scenes are plentiful and handled with a matter-of-fact explicitness, and Barrows never sensationalizes the sordid underworld he writes about. In the end, however, Barrows comes to a familiar conclusion about this life: it is a "self-created hell," and to escape it, he is determined to find a man or woman, having learned that,

> . . . the momentary orgasm of a five-minute acquaintance is self-defeating and I no longer delude myself that love might be found there.
> But the vacuum insists on being filled. I need someone to talk to honestly, to hold, to love, to sleep with and awaken to. . . .

One of the differences between Genet and the American writers he has influenced is his lack of guilt about his homosexuality; he is self-sufficient in his fantasy world. Genet writes about hoodlums because they provide erotic stimulation for him, but most American writers dealing with a similar *milieu* emphasize how guilty they feel about its attractions. Once again puritanism tacks its little moral onto erotic writing: homosexuality is wrong, and it should only be portrayed as ugly and sordid. Genet showed American writers how to write beautifully of homosexual eroticism while retaining their guilt feelings about it: by emphasizing sordidness.

It is a relief to escape from these guilt-ridden narratives into a world of sunlight and good sense, the world d'Arcangelo celebrates in *The Homosexual Handbook,* and his novel, *Sookey* (1969). The *Handbook* amply fulfills the promise of the blurb on the jacket of the original edition:

> Being an Introduction to the Arts, Crafts and Sports, and to the History, Sociology and Philosophy of Masculine Love—Also Courtship and Marriage between Males—designed to Amuse, Enlighten and Instruct all Manner of Readers.

Most guides to subjects sexual, even the most chipper, are inevitably dreary because while they may enlighten and instruct, they fail to amuse. D'Arcangelo is usually amusing, perhaps because of the writing *persona* he adopts for himself: he is the mature sensualist, the worldly-wise and witty "Uncle Fudge" offering advice to less knowledgeable gay readers on subjects ranging from the arts, morals, religion, and society to the techniques of sex and the prevention of venereal disease. Stylistically, he moves from a tone of eighteenth-century elegance to contemporary archness, often on the same page. That the reader remains interested in whatever d'Arcangelo has to say on any topic is a tribute to his unsentimental clear-headedness, as when he carefully separates love from sex, in this passage:

> Love. It's fine, of course. But suppose you don't have the inclination or the time? Why, fuck anyway. Everybody will be better off for it. Desire belongs to the body. Romance afflicts the mind.

Interspersing advice from "Uncle Fudge" (written in response to mock Dear Abby letters) with personal reminiscences and digressions where appropriate, d'Arcangelo is able to charm both homosexual and heterosexual readers without compromising his insistence on the legitimacy and joyfulness of homosexuality. Although many homosexual writers continued to weight their novels with gloom, after the *Handbook* and Amory's *Loon* novels guilt ceased to be a crippling factor in homosexual erotic fiction. The gutter lost its appeal as society reluctantly began to tolerate homosexuality.

A collection of d'Arcangelo's journalistic pieces—mostly taken from underground newspapers like *Gay* and *Screw*—appeared in 1971 with the ambitious title of *Angelo D'Arcangelo's Love Book: Inside the Sexual Revolution from Women's Lib to Gay Power*. Predictably, considering that they were written at the height of the sexual revolution, when homosexuals were first becoming politicized, these pieces are mostly political, and of ephemeral interest; a record by a good journalist of what happened when the closets opened and thousands of gay men and women poured into the streets.

The Turkish Bath (1969) by "Juliette and Justine Lemercier" is the lesbian counterpart of *The Homosexual Handbook*. One half its authorship has been attributed to d'Arcangelo, but it isn't in the same class with *The Homosexual Handbook*. Women talk in dialogue form, advice is offered and stories are told, but it is as dull as one of Sade's dialogues, lacking d'Arcangelo's wit and charm.

Sookey is d'Arcangelo's sole erotic novel. *Sookey* is excellent when the author sticks to describing the *amours* of a gay writer spending the summer on Fire Island. The novel loses focus when he abandons strict realism for flights of romantic fancy which are not integrally connected to the main story. The book should be read for its homosexual erotic scenes; their vividness makes up for the high sugar content found elsewhere.

Before the appearance of *The Homosexual Handbook*, gay readers had to look far and wide for a writer who felt guiltless enough to simply entertain. They found him in Richard Amory, whose extremely popular *Song of the Loon* fantasy series is described by d'Arcangelo:

> Can you imagine *The Last Of The Mohicans* as a gay novel? What about *Hiawatha*? Can you visualize an explora-

tory expedition into the wilds of the northwest, stumbling into a hidden valley of perpetual springtime populated by Indians, white trappers, renegade blacks, and varicolored cowpokes, all camping together in perfect harmony?

If you can, then you've also visualized the world of *Willow Song* (1974), a typical Amory fantasy. In this one a man named Strickland ("Alor," to his primitive lovers) is seduced away from his everyday life by a tree-man named Wilghe, whom he follows willingly,

> His mind's eye filled with memories of frenetic darkness, of hard angles and plain meanings, and he was glad to be rid of them. Not that he understood Wilghe at all or had even the faintest notion of the future path, but he was glad to be rid of certain people . . . and anxious to explore the ways of the willow man, of the alders, of live oaks and buckeyes.

into this vision of Eden:

> He came out into a deep, brilliantly tawny ravine. Long-needled, sage-green pines swept up the hillside, and madrones, and moss-hung live oaks; below, the topaz sparkle of a stream winding through willows and alders and dogwoods. . . .

In order to get to this magic world it is necessary to suspend critical judgment and follow a handsome bronze primitive inside a tree; Amory's readers have found the trip worth the price—a purple, poeticized prose which records lovemaking as "They twined"—because he does not agonize about the homosexuality of his fantasy creatures. His is a special world, like Tolkien's, hermetically sealed from the harshness of reality.

It must be said that when the reader returns from Amory's version of Eden for homosexual men, he is likely to have second thoughts about Amory's saccharine style. But if the *Loon* books are bonbons for the mind, Amory shows in his "gay thriller" *Frost* (1973) that he can serve up heartier fare—and that he knows the politics of guilt as well as any homosexual erotic writer.

Frost begins interestingly enough with an encounter between a young, junior-college Spanish teacher named Frost and a father he hates. The father, McGraw, presses an unlikely job on Frost when he gives him some nude photos of a young man and tells his son to find the man. Pressured into doing detective work for his father, Frost begins to look for the young man by questioning a simple-minded male hustler he hires for sex, a scene described in typical Amory fashion:

> Frost clenched his eyes shut and conjured up his old, first vision of Billy—more real sometimes than the flesh-and-blood body writhing now on top of him—his vision—Billy, an ecstatic Arcadian shepherd on a sunlit hillside; sensitive, poetic, a part of the earth, growing out of warmth like a golden tree, sharing dark, sweet secrets of curly-haired loins and deep, red-warm caverns, while muscle and bone and soft, crinkly hair swept down Frost's body in a summer storm of hard arms and tangling thighs and sweet, probing tongue.

The trail takes him to Billy's murder, through various sexual encounters like the above, and back to his father, the villain of the piece. In the climactic scene between Frost and his homosexual-hating father, Amory inserts an affirmation of homosexuality designed to bring cheers from his gay readers. *Frost* demonstrates that Amory can write an entertaining thriller unlike his *Song* books, make it erotic —and healthily so—without sacrificing the charm that is his main appeal.

Because of its superficiality, it is difficult to treat Amory's work as serious erotic literature. It was designed for popular appeal, just as *The Sexual Adventures of Sherlock Holmes* (1971) by "J. Watson" was. This novel is an amusing *pastiche* of the Holmes stories, entertaining and sometimes convincing in its parody of the original model. Holmes is gay, of course, as is Dr. Watson, and even Mrs. Hudson is revealed to be a man beneath her Victorian dress.

On this popular level but in a more realistic vein are Dirk Vanden's *All* novels: *I Want It All* (1970), *All or Nothing* (1971) and *All Is Well* (1971).

Warren Miller, the protagonist of *I Want It All*, is a cowboy in Colorado who saves a homosexual passing through his small town from a gang rape. In the process he discovers his own homosexuality, and travels to San Francisco where he finds a male lover and a gay world that welcomes him. Vanden is good at taking the reader step by step through the stages of "coming out" and his protagonist is so normal —so awfully sincere—that the reader never loses empathy for him, even when he becomes a male hustler for a few weeks and gets involved in some of the more sordid aspects of gay life. Warren's conclusions about his transformation are summed up by his lover at the end of the book: ". . . love and sex are two completely separate things!" This attitude—so different from the romantic agony of the classic gay novel—is expressed in most of the new homosexual erotic novels; Vanden's protagonists are seen first hating their homosexuality and then arriving at a healthy acceptance of it.

Vanden's second novel, *All or Nothing*, begins at the same time *I Want It All* does: the gang rape of a transient homosexual in a small western town. In *All or Nothing* the protagonist, Bill Thorne, discovers his homosexuality during the rape, just as his friend Warren did. Like Warren, Bill leaves for San Francisco's gay world, and once again Vanden's awkward sincerity makes the reader an accomplice in his protagonist's self-discovery. Vanden's ability to create believable characters in a believable environment—"straight" cowboys in a small western town—and then delineate their transformation in a totally different environment, is valuable in eliciting a sympathetic response from his readers.

All Is Well, the final volume of the trilogy, repeats the basic story of the first two. A "straight" husband and father is followed through his journey to self-acceptance as a homosexual. It is a better-realized, more thoughtful version of the basic *All* storyline. Vanden's touching evocation of male comradeship is one of the strongest elements in his novels. He writes about gay life realistically and even propagandistically, the latter because the reader finds himself believing—as the author intends—that gay men can be warmer and more tender with each other than heterosexuals.

Screw 22 (1969) by Jeff Lawton is that rarity in homosexual erotic fiction: an amusing novel about being gay—in, of all places, the United States Army. Lawton starts from Joseph Heller's premise that everything is SNAFU in the army, and in a vulgar, boisterous, experimental style, makes fun of both homosexuality and the military.

Private Boy (1975) by Rafe Blasi was originally titled *Nothing to It* by the author, but—as so often happens in the genre, his publisher changed the title. Blasi's first two erotic novels showed promise, and *Private Boy* is even a little better, a competent, unpretentious version of the *All* theme. George and Miranda are an average married couple living in Los Angeles. He's in movies, and she's a social worker. Their sex life is good, but George finds himself taking an interest in male bodies, and as his marriage with Miranda comes apart, he recognizes that he is bisexual and possibly homosexual. *Private Boy* is a good example of the kind of homosexual genre novel now being published. Like Vanden's novels, its very typicality shows how far gay fiction has developed since *Finisterre.*

It is hardly surprising that homosexual erotic writers have tended to react to the anti-homosexual attitude of society by writing books that are more valuable as sociology than literature; homoerotic works of artistic merit are few enough that they stand out in bold relief from "message" books by d'Arcangelo, Amory, and Vanden. One of them is *The Tides of Lust* (1973) by Samuel R. Delany.

Samuel R. Delany has a high reputation in the science/speculative fiction genre on the basis of some dozen books, among them *Nova, Driftglass,* and *Dahlgren.* His novels are highly stylized romances, reflecting the imagination of a man who is an omnivorous reader of modern poetry. *The Tides of Lust* is Delany's first erotic novel and the most powerful of all his books. Delany is impatient with the traditional paraphernalia of science fiction. His attitude is obviously the same in regard to the conventions of erotic writing. What he cares about is constructing stories from fragments of colored glass.

There is an urgency in *The Tides of Lust* that isn't found in Delany's other novels. Here he has something to say—devils to exorcise, perhaps—and means to persuade us of his seriousness. More so than in most erotic novels, all the characters in *Tides of Lust* seem but different aspects of one character, the author: there is the black Captain on whose boat, *The Scorpion,* travel two children, Kirsten and Gunner, bought in India by the Captain for sexual service; an artist, Proctor, who has enjoyed every sexual experience; Catherine, a countess, mysterious, fatal; and Robby, a drifter who becomes the catalyst for the climactic scene of the novel.

The story is not complicated, although Delany's language can be. The Captain brings his boat into port, meets Proctor and Robby, and embarks with them and a few other people on a sexual voyage given added significance by Delany's technique of casting flashbacks in the form of reminiscences supposedly written by his characters. Incest, rape, masturbation, urolagnia, sodomy, necrophilia—every variety of sexual appetite is delineated with a savagery rarely seen in erotic novels. Delany puts an innate delicacy of intelligence at the service of a corrosive anger expressive of every brutal pornographic fantasy.

The role of the artist is a major theme:

> . . . Man has devised three systems for effecting the
> oblivion necessary for sanity. First, the whole bourgeois pre-
> occupation—such a very good word, "preoccupy"—with work
> and the objects of its reward. Second, the religious erection
> —ahem—of a moral, ethical, and ritual matrix that must ab-
> sorb man's consciousness to be efficacious. And third is the
> erotic life in which we have chosen to submerge ourselves.
> I say we; more accurately, you. The artist is perhaps the only
> one free to indulge in all three, religious, erotic, and ergonic,
> simply to fulfill his calling. He reports to the practitioners
> of each what is going on within the circles of the others.
> That is why society supports him, I suppose. And they are
> all, always, so fascinated to learn.

That is Proctor, explaining the role of the erotic artist,
which Delany very consciously is in *The Tides of Lust*. He is
romantic, artificial, very aware that he is the poet making
myth out of his fantasies, but the sum of this artifice is a
powerful erotic novel in which sexual categories are rendered meaningless.

> One does not write to be understood. One does not write
> to entertain. The artist's greatest value is, like the criminal's,
> that he is concerned with symmetry first and values only sub-
> ordinately.

A novel by the playwright Ronald Tavel (*Chelsea Girls,
Boy on the Straight-Back Chair*) entitled *Street of Stairs* was
published in 1968 by The Olympia Press in a version which
cut out sixty percent of the manuscript. What was printed
contains the story of a love affair set in Tangier between a
young American expatriate named Mark and a Moroccan
thief and killer named Hamid. By virtue of Tavel's remarkable narrative—told by forty different characters speaking
various dialects in an *Arabian Nights* collection of brief stories
—Tangier itself becomes the protagonist of the book. The
book glitters with a dense poetry that is the perfect preserva-
tive for capturing the sensuality and aimless violence beneath

ordered tradition found in North Africa. The love story between Mark and Hamid assumes legendary outlines because of Tavel's evocative, stylistic inventiveness. Tangier becomes a symbol—as it does in Paul Bowles' fiction—of an erotic heart of darkness, and Tavel's characters travel to the center of its mystery. *Street of Stairs* had at one time a considerable underground reputation, although it seems to have been forgotten since its publication. If the complete manuscript is ever published, it will claim its rightful place—on sheer literary merit—as one of the most beautiful of homosexual erotic novels.

Leo Skir's *Boychick* (1971) is an autobiographical novel about a gay graduate student who falls in love with a hard-hearted young boy he calls "boychick." The situation is so conventional it would be painful without Skir's self-mocking precision of language. His protagonist, Leo Tsalis, has devouring Jewish parents who are paying his way through N.Y.U. Graduate School; Leo is interested in Old English and Spenser, has an apartment of his own, and falls in love (of a qualified sort, no grand passion here, indeed no overstatement anywhere in the novel) with a boy he sees in the shower at the St. George Hotel pool in Brooklyn Heights.

> While I was taking a shower I noticed a blond boy outside the shower stall. He looked about fourteen or fifteen. . . . "Now, Leo," I said to myself, "that is a *boy*. You have a bad mind."

The rest of the novel is an account of Leo's attempts to see boychick and get him into bed, although he proceeds so timidly the narrative becomes less of a progress toward seduction than the pursuit of a medieval dream figure. Yet we see little of the dream, and a lot of Leo's friends, parents, and the grotesque people he picks up in bars. *Boychick* is a determinedly cool self-portrait of a surprisingly winning protagonist: Leo is ironic, self-deprecatory, spare, and self-revealing when it is least expected. He can also be obnoxious, and an estimation of the merits of *Boychick* will depend largely on the reader's response to him.

Obsession (1970) by George Hayim is about the obsessive nature of a sadomasochistic relationship between a middle-aged member of the jet set named Jo and a young boy named Edouard. Edouard subjects Jo to sadistic miseries, but Jo responds with a humor and unfailing patience, happy to assume a subordinate role to his brutal young lover so long as he can be near him. The sincerity of Jo's obsession is poignantly manifested in Hayim's restrained narration, such as when he describes buying sheets for Edouard.

> . . . It had all been worthwhile—the drama, the agony, the madness. He would be with me at last.
> I started by buying sheets for him. My idea was to get things that would later be of use in his new apartment in Paris. . . . These sheets were to be used for him and me now, and later? For him and his wife? Edouard was right, what I did for him was for me, and me alone.

The sadomasochistic theme of *Obsession* is so discreetly presented that it can serve as an introduction to two novels, one masterly and one trashy, which deal much more directly with the role of sadomasochism in homosexual erotic litererature. *The Real Thing* (1968) by William Carney is without doubt a masterpiece of erotic literature. *Run, Little Leather Boy* (1971) by Larry Townsend is typical of popular gay fiction with a sadomachistic theme. What these two very different books have in common is a perspective which insists that SM is not a sexual deviation, but an approach to life itself, as the critic Alan Hull Walton suggests in his introduction to *The Real Thing*. Both authors seek to establish this view of SM by describing it as another world, ruled by a strict morality. In *Run, Little Leather Boy* we follow the sexual adventures of a spoiled, wealthy young man named Wayne Hoffsteder as he discovers first, that he is a homosexual, and second, that he is attracted by the discipline of master and slave. When his parents send him off to his uncle in England because of his sexual misconduct at home, his uncle, far from being a "good influence" on Wayne, becomes his guide to the subtleties of sadomasochism. When Wayne suggests that SM is a game, his uncle enlightens him.

> "For many, unfortunately, it is," sighed Bert. "For the purist, it is not. It is, as I have already noted, an art—a skill one develops until he is able to fulfill his own and his partner's fantasies by enactment of the role as set forth by the tacit or stated agreement between himself and that partner. It is all performed within prescribed limits, you see, and the limits are established for each encounter. There is really no game. For us it is life, and the opportunity to activate the most profound potentials within our living minds and bodies."

These sentiments are elaborated into a philosophy of life by the professorial uncle of *The Real Thing,* whose letters to a nephew interested in sadomasochism comprise the narrative of this epistolary novel. Like Lord Chesterfield writing letters of advice to his nephew, the author of these instructions to a novitiate is witty, precise, and elegant —and very certain of the moral values implicit in his revolutionary morality. In a detached, avuncular tone he patiently initiates his nephew into the rituals and philosophy of his discipline. Through his eyes we follow his nephew's growth to mastery—and to the *denouement* of the book, the encounter between two artists of pain. The appeal of *The Real Thing* is solely to the intellect; unlike Townsend, Carney does not dwell on specifically sexual situations. Carney is allusive, subtle, and utterly persuasive in his argument that sadomasochism is indeed an approach to life where what matters is the creation of an orderly world, in which people are seen not humanistically, but realistically.

> I found that all friendship, whether accidental, social, or hospitable, can become erotic. I found that the only work-

able relationship possible between human beings was a pack hierarchy of roles in the play of abandonment, search, submission, and mastery. I found that all people are to a greater or lesser extent fugitives from justice of one sort or another, real or imagined, and are covertly seeking retribution, and the way I chose to follow is the one which finds them out. Here is personal punishment guided by no impersonal agency, but directed rather by the human hand, *a real and living hand* capable of at once caressing and killing; punishment intoned in a private litany and guided by a disciplined heart. Yes! the heart! It is a stern affection, but very real nevertheless—and more strengthening than any other this life has to offer.

I found that suffering does indeed imply guilt. Put your finger on the hidden guilt and you increase at once the suffering and a need to discharge the source of it, which is a myth. Thus discharged, the pleasure principle takes over and there is victimhood, the candidate in his white robe, waiting. . . .

As we have seen in what d'Arcangelo calls the "classic Gay Novel" guilt plays an inordinately large role in homosexual erotic writing; the fascination with criminals and the lowlife *milieu* found in novels by Genet's American cousins stems in part from the same emotion. *The Real Thing* returns to this theme, but Carney, like Genet, establishes his own moral system separate from ours, a system in which guilt finds its outlet in ritual. At this point homosexual erotic literature seems to be moving away from guilt toward the creation of alternate, enclosed worlds like Amory's or Carney's where homosexuality is the norm. Although this may be attributed to reaction against the heterosexual order of things—an order which has rejected homosexual eroticism— it is certainly preferable to the guilty anguish of earlier homo-erotic novels. But whether the vision is utopian or sado-masochistic, the homosexual erotic novel of the future will turn away from guilt to celebrate the joys of the flesh and the mysteries of the spirit.

XI

THE METASEXUAL NOVELIST

> To fuck, this is all we know and all
> we derive from. The rest is food,
> clothing, and shelter. And all the ac-
> complishments of our civilizations,
> every last work of religion or art or
> science, has been nothing but a frip-
> pery to pass the time away, to keep
> oneself busy while one was not do-
> ing the only thing in which human
> beings achieve totality: fucking.
> —MARCO VASSI

ALONE AMONG American erotic writers, Marco Vassi has attempted to formulate a philosophy of eroticism. Although he
has written nine books, some of them banal and some of
them brilliant—all of which demonstrate his ability to recreate the sexual moment vividly and truthfully—it is not
his imagination but the power of his ideas that makes him
the most interesting figure in recent erotic literature. He is

primarily a didactic artist who asks the question, how are we to live? and answers: by eroticizing our lives. For Vassi, it is our sexuality that makes us human. Eroticism is the secret center of our beings, "a vast river which sustains a mighty jungle."

The apocalyptic note has been sounded, by a man who addresses us with D. H. Lawrence's passionate certitude. It is a note which reverberates through Vassi's best books, and if at times it seems strident, it is never insincere. Vassi is the only erotic writer since Georges Bataille to express his perceptions about eroticism along philosophical lines. Because of the seriousness of these ideas and the range of his nine books—autobiography, fables, sexual manifestos, superior erotic fiction, essays, and formula genre novels—a detailed examination of his work and thought should yield a definitive and representative portrait of the modern erotic writer and the literature he creates.

Metasexuality is the central concept in his writings, a term which he uses to mean pure eroticism—sexuality separated from its reproductive context. Metasexuality does away with categories like homosexuality, heterosexuality, bisexuality and perversions replacing them with sexual modes: theatrical, masturbatory, romantic, therapeutic, and procreative.

Vassi explains the metasexual concept in his essay, "The Metasexual Manifesto," included in the book *Metasex, Mirth & Madness* (1975).

> Sex is biological, metasex is psychophysical. Sex, the biological eroticum, is for procreation and for no other reason; metasex, the psychophysical eroticum, is for any other reason whatsoever. Metasexually, there is no real difference between what two men do in bed, from what three women might do in bed, nor from what a man and woman do in bed.

The metasexual idea was introduced in Vassi's first novel, *Mind Blower* (1970). It is an awkward novel, suffering from woodenness of plot, characterization, and dialogue, more interesting for its ideas and its erotic scenes than as the story of a young man named Michael who, desiring to "get in touch with people who were playing serious sexual games," answers an ad in *The New York Times* asking for an assistant to a master of arcane studies. When he goes to an interview for the position, he meets an extraordinary fat man named Doctor Tocco, who heads the Institute For Sexual Metatheatre. Tocco shocks him *("It is the shock which teaches")* by insisting that he make love to a young girl even before they talk. Afterwards, he asks:

> Are you sure you want to go on, to pursue this knowledge, into the mysteries of sex and its partner, death, to follow the terrifying paths of beauty and terror to their final end?

Michael is a familiar figure in erotic fiction: the seeker of erotic knowledge. He has come to Tocco because of dissatisfaction with his own sexuality—he has never achieved complete union in sex with anyone because he and his partners have never shared the same fantasies—and he accepts Tocco's challenge. The remainder of the novel is the narrative of Michael's progress toward erotic enlightenment. Tocco calls Michael's various sexual experiments "role actualization." By acting out every fantasy, subtle or monstrous, Michael is able to shed his individuality like old skin. Tocco explains this to Michael:

> This gets to the core of metatheatre. For every facet of our beloved personality, every thought, every mood, every attitude, every value, every conviction, is nothing but the flimsiest stage trapping, and if a human being is to have true inner dignity, he or she must be able to put on and take off these psychological costumes with the ease of changing a hat or a pair of gloves.

Such ideas, combined with superb erotic scenes, keep the reader's attention from straying on occasions in *Mind Blower* when careless writing and plotting become distracting; the reader's—and Michael's—reward for perseverance is a glowing vision of erotic union.

> I felt as though my ego had dissolved and come together again, but now it had four faces instead of the one, and it was impossible for me to tell the difference between any of us. In the realest sense of the word, we were all one person. And anything one of us felt, all of us felt. The room seemed to hum with a soft vibration, and we were lifted by a kind of psychic elevator which took us from the world of mundane perceptions to a world where everything was washed clean, and was always fresh, always being born, always coming into awareness of itself.

For Vassi, ego transcendence is only achieved by people strong enough to descend into the frightening, uncharted depths of eroticism, people strong enough to discard conventional sexual morality, who recognized that:

> In our society, everything is a lie. You walk down the street and look at the jiggling breasts and tight-skirted asses and in five minutes there are a dozen women you want to fuck and who would like nothing better than to be fucked. But you are not allowed to do it. Moreover, you are not even allowed to think it. You censor yourself. Everyone is afraid. Everyone lies.

Because this book is not about sex but rather the literature of sex, we have focused, up to now, on those aspects of erotic writing which can be criticized according to the standards applied to general literature. But there is very little precedent for the literary appreciation of erotic description. These scenes are implanted like time bombs within the pages of erotic novels. People get jittery about them.

They fail to see some obvious parallels between the function of sexual description in erotic writing and the description of other human activities in non-erotic literature. As an example of these parallels, look again at the mystery story. Although we cannot pretend that the erotic novelist's description of sexual activities is the exact equivalent of the mystery writer's description of murder—because people read erotic novels primarily to be aroused by sexual descriptions, and mystery stories not to see murder described but a puzzle solved—nevertheless murder plays the same role in mystery novels that sex does in erotic novels. It is difficult to understand how people who object to reading the novelist's blow by blow description of love-making can read with equanimity the scenes of violent death that play so large a role not only in mystery novels, but in war literature, and indeed, in most of twentieth-century writing.

Because of its range, Vassi's work affords us an opportunity to look more closely at the function of sexual description in erotic writing. It is important, it is central; but the argument of this book is that erotic writing offers the reader intellectual and even spiritual rewards aside from the obvious pleasures of sexual description, and so I have waited until a context was created in which it could be viewed in proportion to these other qualities. In this perspective, erotic scenes in writing must seem legitimate portrayals of the most basic of human activities. Calmly viewed, erotic scenes are, on the most mundane level, simply physical description; on the highest level, they are capable of recreating that heightened moment during sex when we perceive the oneness of all things.

The scene that follows from *Mind Blower* falls somewhere in between these extremes. Tocco explains to Michael that he is going to witness the enactment of a sexual fantasy. The fantasist is a woman who wants to be gang-raped, in a bit of sexual metatheatre. It is shocking, both to Michael and the reader; but the rape is necessary to the woman, and its description is necessary to the book. Tocco first explains the woman's fantasy.

"Here we have the archetypal cockteaser, the woman who holds the favor of her burgeoning body in promise to all men and yet gives her favors to none. She is a tense, castrating bitch, and that is but a cover for a frightened teenage girl. She is walking home alone late one night. Suddenly she turns a corner and is grabbed and whisked into a room. Inside the room are eight men who have had no sex for weeks. It's an interesting bit of drama, don't you think?"

What happens next is a censor's nightmare, but remember the context in which it takes place: it is voluntary sexual theater and its goal is the transcendence of the ego.

At once they were all upon her, putting their fingers and hands into her cunt, reaching and digging between her legs, going into her asshole, spreading her legs wider and wider. The man went back to saying things in her ear again, and again her face contracted in a strange kind of pain. But as she sobbed "no" to him, she kicked up her legs, grabbed her ankles with her hands, and spread her legs as wide apart as they would go.

They swarmed over her like ants. For a moment she was almost lost from sight. And then some definite action began to emerge, as one after the other of them moved around to lick or bite or kiss different parts of her body. . . .

We will look at several of these scenes in Vassi's work. Although there is no need to dwell on them, it is necessary to understand and accept their function in erotic fiction. In the passage quoted, the emphasis is on the fantasy of being forced and degraded, but the goal of the woman's fantasy enactment is suggested by the sentence, "They swarmed over her like ants." For a moment, she loses her unhappy individual identity and becomes simply flesh to be used and merged with other flesh. Vassi is not an assaultive writer of erotic scenes; even when the sex is brutal, as in this passage, his intention is not to shock but to recall with exactitude each erotic movement, while remaining faithful to the emotional truth of the situation.

In *Mind Blower,* the protagonist learns the necessity of denying love itself, of seeing that tenderness is an emotion no better or worse than others, because emotional attachments inhibit his progress to erotic enlightenment. He becomes detached, able to change psychological masks at will. He denies that any of them is more important than the next, because then he would be trapped within a biological sex role. Metasexuality requires that its practitioners give no more weight to one emotion than another.

This Zen-like attitude is illustrated by the actions of the protagonists in Vassi's second and third novels, *The Gentle Degenerates* (1970) and *The Saline Solution* (1971). The opening sentences of *The Gentle Degenerates* make the announcement:

> There is love, which is neither personal nor impersonal; and there is sex, which is either personal or impersonal. We love, and want to fuck. But we fuck, and so often love disappears. . . .

The speaker at the beginning of this novel is in a love relationship with a woman named Regina. Although he believes in sexual freedom, he is a jealous man, and when Regina leaves him to go to California he is relieved that he won't have to suffer any longer the pangs of jealousy or the trap of marriage. He is free to explore impersonal sex. The remainder of the novel describes the narrator's sexual encounters with various women as he tries on one sexual mask after another, always looking for that ultimate union that he knows exists, although he despairs of finding it.

Vassi draws portraits of hellish marriages torn apart by a constant questioning of their basic premises. When his narrator is free of a love relationship, he is free to lead a metasexual life in which eroticism is the only value. Vassi's intimate knowledge of the subtle interplay between men and women, and his honesty with himself (for all his work is autobiographical, like Henry Miller's) help in part to redeem an unattractive self-obsession manifested in the attitude that other people and their emotions are of value only insofar as they help him learn how to live. His attitude is impersonal, indifferent to the conventional values placed on things: it is the ruthlessness of the explorer. This is what he discovers about marriage:

> Then I understood what I could never get clear with Regina, that specialness between two human beings is always an *ad hoc* contract. It is made on pure impulse, and has no justification other than its own existence. When either or both of the parties feel it disappear or drive it away, then it no longer exists, and there can be no recriminations. Also, it has nothing to say about sexual activities with others. Somehow, between two people, a special kind of flow is possible, and when that is there, there are no rules about anything else. . . .

But even in such a relationship impersonality remains of strategic importance:

> The reason sex gets boring in marriage is that both partners forget how to be impersonal with one another.

For Vassi, relationships are above all learning experiences; no matter how intense his feelings for a woman are, he is separate from her except during sex.

Vassi bothers very little with plot or characterization in his novels. He is a didactic artist, an explorer of eroticism with findings to present; like most such writers from Sade onward, his narrative only serves as a vehicle for the exposition of his ideas. Typically, he will begin with a basic situation—the Institute for Sexual Metatheatre in *Mind Blower,* the break-up of a marriage in *The Gentle Degenerates,* an abortion in *The Saline Solution*—and the remainder of the novel will consist of a series of sexual encounters meant to illustrate and further his argument. This lack of structure may be ascribed in part to the formula Vassi followed when The Olympia Press was his publisher—fifty percent of a novel had to be sexual description and the other half was his to do with as he pleased—but his impatience with the techniques of fiction is as much to blame.

Ruthlessness is at the heart of *The Saline Solution:* the protagonist is obviously Vassi himself, and this time the woman he has a relationship with is pregnant. As in *The Gentle Degenerates,* the basic situation of the novel is announced in the opening lines:

> We didn't know whether we wanted the baby, so we drifted in indecision until Lucinda passed the third month of pregnancy. And then it became a question of murder.
> It was to have been a casual affair of impersonal intensity. . . .

Vassi has said that the conflict in all his work is that of approach-avoidance, and his statement is borne out by the struggle in each of his novels between the desire to live within a relationship and an even stronger desire to be free of it. He is speaking of marriage when he says

> The most invidious myth of our civilization is the idea that any form of social contract can substitute for unrelenting moment-to-moment awareness by each individual. Lucinda and I attempted to laugh in the face of necessity by assuming a relationship in which all the emotional glue of attachment would be dissolved by acid sophistication. . . .

Later in the novel, he expands on this notion:

> The couple is the insignia of civilization rampant. . . . From some false concept of relationship, some erroneous notion of what a family is, have come the good citizens, the upright parishioners, the fodder for convents and armies, the grease for the gears of civil law. . . .

In each of Vassi's novels politics and history are interpreted in the context of eroticism: the world is in the sad mess it's in because people live not from their erotic centers, but according to the demands of their cultures.

The Saline Solution is the record of a summer spent on Fire Island, during the time when the narrator and Lucinda are trying to decide whether or not to have the baby she is carrying. In the end she makes the decision by herself, and decides to have an abortion. Vassi follows this relationship with Lucinda through the book, and his choice of details once again demonstrates his ability to reveal the erotic subtleties of male-female relationships as few writers since D. H. Lawrence have done. Naturally, there are affairs with other women, but in this novel what had only been tangential in the first two books—the narrator's homosexuality—is presented as an alternative to heterosexual relationships. Increasingly, his protagonists turn to other men:

> . . . The man mood was on me again. And I wanted to yield, not to analyze. After all the years of battling with labels, I know that any attempted judgment of sexual behavior was stupid. And yet there was no peace. Was my desire for men an escape from my inability to make it with a woman, my fear of having a child? Or was my repeated effort at marriage a refusal to face the fact of my basic homosexuality?

Part of the complexity of Vassi's autobiographical *persona* arises from this conflict between sex roles. Although he espouses metasexuality, he agonizes over his biological sexuality. He is at times *macho,* jealous, possessive, chauvinistic, and even misogynistic, and these feelings make for painful heterosexual relationships. Frustrated, he seeks escape in impersonal sex with both women and men. He attempts to transcend his biological sex role with all its drawbacks by becoming just the opposite of it. Unity is found only during sex, and his erotic scenes often indicate this.

> I lowered myself onto her. All the bulges down the front of me found hollows along her back to nestle in. My knees into the backs of her knees, her buttocks into my groin, my belly into the small of her back, my chest on her spine. I

reached under her and worked one breast into each of my hands, feeling the thick pleasure of the soft glandular pressure of her tits. I relaxed my full weight on her and we tacitly abandoned ourselves to the exclusivity of one another's satisfaction. It was as though fucking were a truce, a spacetime in which we could allay alienation and find a temporary comfort in the union of our physical communication. In fucking, the language is basic, the dualities are clear: yes, no; brutal, tender; in, out; aggression, passivity; and on down the entire ontology of experience. In fucking, the play of mood captures at least the form, if not the essence, of an extended gesture, which subsumes music, incorporates dance, and attains to poetry.

Vassi's fourth novel, *Contours of Darkness* (1972) is his longest and most ambitious. It is, in fact, the first that seems truly fictional in the sense that it has more than one major character, is told in the third person, attempts a broader scope than in previous books, and possesses a skeletal plot. Yet somehow when Vassi abandons his usual autobiographical method, clarity is sacrificed. *Contours of Darkness* is another attempt to come to terms with the themes of the first three books, particularly the problem of relationship, but it has lost the sharp ruthless focus of the autobiographical novels.

Aaron is a school teacher in Berkeley, California, married to Cynthia, who is perhaps more prepared for sexual freedom in their marriage than Aaron. Their friend Conrad is a radical student of nineteen, twelve years Aaron's junior. The three friends become lovers, and as their freedom expands, they include homosexual and lesbian relationships. Vassi's recurrent theme of the difficulty of relationships is explored once again, against the background of the radical politics of the late sixties. Although there is talk of revolution by Weatherman-type radicals, and Conrad is jailed at the end of the novel for his activities, the answer to the problems faced by the characters is not political:

The civilization you talk about destroying is some abstract monster out there; it exists inside us, it is us. . . .

Aaron and Cynthia separate by the end of the book, Cynthia to pursue political ends while Aaron is left to tend his own garden, feeling himself a failure as both husband and revolutionary. Yet Vassi's conclusion about political revolution—despite the attention paid to radical politics by his characters—seems unchanged from previous novels. The only real revolution is of consciousness.

. . . The true revolution lies in the mutation of consciousness that takes place in individuals, and for a woman —as for a man—that quest must bring her, sooner or later, to the limits she places on her definition of her own sexuality.

As if to demonstrate that he has not arrived at these conclusions about the importance of eroticism easily, Vassi published a non-erotic autobiography, *The Stoned Apocalypse*, in 1972. In it he describes his Catholic upbringing in the Italian slums of East Harlem, a tour of duty in Japan for the Air Force, and editorial jobs that left him unsatisfied with his life. Beginning from that point he describes flirtations with Communism, Scientology, Gurdjieffian therapy, and the sensory awareness groups which sprang up in California in the late sixties. The book follows his efforts to wake up from the sleep of ordinary existence and ends in near-madness. Having decided not to kill himself to escape the conflicts within him, he becomes a pornographer.

And shortly thereafter I plugged in to the current of sexual flow which increases in intensity and volume in inverse proportion to the level of conscious freedom in the nation. I added a new mask to the theater of identifications and became a pornographer. . . .

There is only what is, and that is mute. *I have stopped searching.*

Although it is not an erotic book, *The Stoned Apocalypse* is necessary reading if one is to realize the full seriousness of Vassi's thesis that an end to conflict is found only in the context of metasexual eroticism. *The Stoned Apocalypse* is evidence that his quest has not been limited to sexuality and so gives an extra dimension to his conclusions.

The French Job (1973) was originally titled *Hot Type* by the author. It is something of a *roman à clef*, based on Vassi's knowledge of publishers who specialize in erotic fiction. Like *Contours of Darkness* it makes more use of the traditional techniques of fiction. It has a fairly large cast of characters whose stories are narrated in the third person, and a fairly cohesive plot. The major characters in the story are Lou Morris, a publisher who enjoys making film records of his sexual experiences with his young female editors, and Joan, a copy editor who plays the role of Justine to a Juliette named Margaret. *The French Job* is superior to conventional genre fiction, but it shares many of its worst characteristics, in this case an overemphasis on erotic scenes. Dialogue and ideas are cut short so that the characters can fall in bed according to formula.

Joan is taken step by step through most of the possible varieties of sex as found in formula erotica: orgies, sex with her boss in order to keep her job, lesbian sex, and lustful urgings for a Puerto Rican mail clerk. What makes *The French Job* superior to its formula is Vassi's talent, and the intrinsic interest of the situation—that the people who publish erotic fiction actually do lead more exciting sex lives than the rest of us. But even this cannot redeem the clichéd language and rigid formulas that, weed-like, choke the novel.

Vassi remains true to his themes, however. The jaded character of Lou Morris seems to echo the Vassi protagonist of the early novels when, after showing Margaret some erotic films, he responds to her objection that the people on the screen are robots.

"The trouble with you," Lou said to her, not taking his eyes off the screen, "is that you're still in the romantic era.

Pornography is in an abstract phase right now. Those people up there aren't to be probed or dissected for their life histories. They are bodies, beautiful bodies in suggestive costumes and interesting poses. And they are doing something quite splendid with their hands and mouths and cocks and cunts and asses. They are giving themselves up to a shared experience. We are witnessing a delicate and charming communion. And there is nothing to identify with except the thing itself. . . ."

That is, sexuality as an end in itself, pure and impersonal, divorced from its emotional and cultural contexts.

Vassi's next novel, *Pro Ball Groupie* (1974) by "Julie Ann DeWitt" fulfills all the requirements of genre fiction, in that nothing more serious happens in it than the erotic scenes specified by formula. The story line has to do with a cheerleader named Julie who gets sexually involved with an entire football team. The dialogue is light and quick, and the plot extends to include every absurdity Vassi dreams up. Despite the obviously banal story line, it is just as obvious that Vassi is playing with the formulas of the genre in *Pro Ball Groupie*. In the process he adds more meaning than is usually found in such novels, as in this passage on the theme of sexual communion.

We sat like that for a very long time, not moving, until our breaths became as gentle as those of a sleeping infant. More than any superficially sexual sensation, I felt a deep and abiding completion, a joining which held intimations of a real union. . . . I entered a state of awareness which soared beyond all words, beyond all meaning, a gentle undifferentiated bliss which in truth had nothing to do with my much-vaunted individuality.

In Touch (1975) marks Vassi's return to serious erotic fiction. The theme of the novel—that one person's fantasy is another's reality—is introduced in a melodramatic but startling first chapter in which a dancer leaps from the top of the World Trade Center building despite the pleas of her therapist, a woman named Lydia. Her patient's death causes Lydia to reexamine her own beliefs about reality, and once she begins that dangerous process she finds herself drawn into a reevaluation of the basic tenets of therapy itself. At an orgy, she is confronted with a view of reality which ultimately becomes her own. A man tells her:

> I choose from whichever frame of reference allows me to move through the flux of creation with as much pleasure and meaning to myself as possible. . . .

But the event which launches Lydia on a voyage to the discovery of her personal reality is the death of her control therapist, a seventy-year-old guru figure who has a heart attack while making love to her. The two deaths propel her into a new approach to therapy in which she encourages her patients to express their fantasies physically.

> I'm beginning to see that once we free our fantasies, they will take us anywhere we want to go. But not just in our heads. They will tell us what we need to know to live well, like fairy tales or parables. And they can change our emotions, and our perception of reality, and even the nature of reality itself. . . .

Lydia's own transformation involves her patients, whom she joins in sexual group encounters, relinquishing her status as their therapist in order to form a new group which is familial in structure and religious in nature. She loses her accreditation as a therapist, but by then it doesn't matter. She and the other members of her new family move to New Mexico to live out their shared fantasy communally. She is visited there by Fred, an old lover, whose skepticism about her new life causes Lydia to push him over a cliff at the moment of orgasm. In the final chapter Vassi tells us that everything that has taken place was part of Fred's dream while sleeping with Lydia: *In Touch* is a shaggy dog story about the nature of reality and illusion.

A collection of essays and erotic fables entitled *Metasex, Mirth & Madness* is a good introduction to Vassi's ideas; here for the first time his most important themes are presented systematically and seductively. They play through the twelve "erotic fables for radical minds" which make up half the book, and are organized into essays and manifestos like "Bodhi is the Body," "Beyond Bisexuality," and "The Metasexual Manifesto."

The fables do not show Vassi at his best as a writer. His subtitle for them, "A Carcass Of Dreams" indicates their adolescent, romantic tone. The first fable in the book, "The Dying Gynecologist" focuses on the last thoughts of a man who became a gynecologist so he could look at female genitals. His past life flashes through his mind, and he dies. The story ends:

> In one of his notebooks there was found the notation, "There are too few doctors who remember the original reason for playing doctor."

The ending is clever, but it doesn't tell us anything we didn't already know. Other fables—"Land Of The Sperm King" based on the idea that "sperm is the perfect food" or "Circus Of Jade" about "the formation of a sexual cyclotron"—are more successful. They accomplish a kind of intellectual seduction: in them, Vassi leads the reader into a frontier world where sexuality is the most important aspect of existence, which is what he has done most consistently in his novels.

Vassi's essays present the thinking of a man who—to his great credit—has worked out a sexual philosophy based on personal experience. He has tested the truth of his conclusions with his own body, and it is to these conclusions we must turn in order to summarize his philosophy.

These seven essays are pungent with the smell of sexual experience. The first, "Bodhi is the Body" begins with the proposition that enlightenment is not a paradisiacal state divorced from moment-to-moment consciousness, but is instead a state of constant awareness; from this insight, Vassi proceeds to build his argument that enlightenment may be found in eroticism, and that women—ignored by all the sages of enlightenment—may teach a man as much as he can learn from any guru.

> . . . what has been denied to women is the acknowledgement that they are teachers of life *in their very bodies*. . . . The sickness of mankind has been the overwhelming importance placed on discursive thinking, to the detriment of the life processes at large. . . .
> Existence is not an idea. It is the air we breathe, the food we eat, the sun that warms us. Only the diseased imaginations of those who are incapable of orgasmic release produce fantasies of a reality other than that which explodes and murmurs within us and without us from moment to moment, on all its planes and levels, endlessly. Reality is known through the trembling awareness of the immediate now, a now which includes all that has been and all that will be.

Referring to a night spent with a woman who taught him "as much as any Zen master," Vassi points to the heart of his philosophy: transcendence of the ego through eroticism.

> . . . There, in the cock and cunt, in the heat and patterns, in the movement and stillness, in the sound and silence, in pervasively private moments when male and female join to become a single entity, is the key to our search for meaning.

Two essays which show Vassi at the height of his ability to communicate ideas by referring to direct sexual experience are "The Trucks" in which he joins a group of anonymous homosexuals for impersonal, uncomplicated sex, and "Bisexuality, Therapy, and Revolution" consisting of thoughts which crystalized during a four-hour period of "fucking-meditation" at a steambath catering to homosexuals. In the latter essay, Vassi refers frequently to Wilhelm Reich's ideas about how fascism is manifested in character structure. The author of *The Function of the Orgasm* has been an important influence on Vassi's work; Vassi considers Reich "the greatest martyr since Giordano Bruno."

> I hold firmly with Reich that the political and military aspects of fascism are the superstructural manifestations of the rigidity of the character formation of the individuals who live in, that is to say, constitute, a fascist state. The enemy is within our own bodies. . . .

It is important to bear in mind that such thoughts arise in this essay during homosexual intercourse. Vassi bears witness to his visions with his body.

In "Beyond Bisexuality" Vassi illustrates how he lost his "sexual identity and became a sexual entity" by referring to lovemaking with another man and a woman. During these triangular relationships he formulates the concept of metasexuality.

> At the far edge of bisexuality I realized that all that had gone before was but the task of perfecting the instrument, the mindbody that is myself. My adventures had served a single purpose: to exhaust all the subjective aspects of the sexual act. The many modes, which had been challenges, areas of exploration, were now my tools—homosexuality, heterosexuality, bisexuality, abstruse psychosexual states and practices, the so-called perversions, the many masks of libidinal displacement . . . these were now at my command, to be used the way a director uses a cast of characters to realize a vision.
>
> Having no term which encompassed the totality of my erotic awareness and function, I found it necessary to coin a new word, and thus formulated the concept: METASEXUALITY.

"The Metasexual Manifesto" is an elaboration of this concept, the main points of which we have touched upon in the preceding pages. It is the single most important essay in Vassi's work because it contains or implies all the major themes of his writing from the beginning to the present.

Just as Vassi's concept of metasexuality encompasses all the forms of eroticism, so his books exhibit the range possible within erotic literature, from genre entertainment to philosophy. He is the most representative of contemporary erotic writers, and certainly the most important philosopher of eroticism in America, for three reasons: his insistence on the primary emotional importance of sexuality; his assault on sexual categorization through the idea of metasexuality; and his vision of the transcendence of the ego through erotic communion.

XII

THE SECRET RECORD

> I believe that the supreme philo-
> sophical question coincides with the
> summits of eroticism.
>
> —GEORGES BATAILLE

THE FUTURE OF EROTIC writing is problematical. In America
its development would seem to be linked to a continued
public interest in exploring the dimensions of sexuality,
an interest that was stimulated by the introspective search
for alternatives in the nineteen-sixties. One of the reasons
why America did not have a native erotic literature of substance until that time may be that historically, Americans
have been outward-looking problem solvers. An optimistic,
successful, and materialistic culture is usually not a reflective
one. But out of the sixties came a small but significant shift

in the national consciousness, which created a receptivity to the demands of our secret selves. People began talking to each other about the quality of their lives. It was a period of inward exploration, when people sought spiritual, political, and emotional alternatives. Sexuality was virtually unexplored territory, to which erotic writers were the only guides.

I have argued in previous chapters that these writers are contributors to a serious form of literary expression with its own traditions and high achievements. Erotic writing exists because it answers a deeply felt need for the public exploration of eros. It expresses for us the secret part of ourselves that most strongly resists the dehumanizing tendencies of the age, as the critic Peter Michelson says in *The Aesthetics Of Pornography* (1971).

> The anarchy implicit in the pornographic genre is not simply an urge to undermine accepted standards, it is the urge to refute them, to demonstrate that they are humanly destructive. That anarchy is itself no antidote only means that the anarchic stage of criticism is preparing the way for creative responses to the placid murderousness of modern culture. . . .

Or, as Marco Vassi says, "eroticism is the humanizing corrective." The erotic writing discussed in this book—formula novel or masterpiece—reminds us of the Dionysian imperative: whether eroticism is expressed anarchically, assaultively, or religiously, the lord of eros will not be denied his awesome role in our lives.

One of the functions of erotic writing is to remind us of this. Erotic writers serve Dionysus, well or badly, depending upon the seriousness with which they approach their subject. We read them intelligently only when we are able to differentiate between bad and good erotic writing, a job that literary critics have for the most part neglected. Only a handful of them have addressed themselves to erotic writing and the problems of criticizing it, among them

Strother Purdy in his essay "On The Psychology Of Erotic Literature," included in *The Perverse Imagination* (1970).

> . . . there has been very little qualitative or scholarly criticism of erotic literature. Social taboo has kept it down, of course—how many learned journals would, or even will, print such studies?—but so has the already mentioned dearth of specialist background studies. We have enough of that critical information now, little enough, but so much more than we had a few years ago that we might get started on the outlines of critical theory in this area.

That critics have not yet gotten started on the outlines of a critical theory in this area is demonstrated by the fact that the essays collected in *The Perverse Imagination* and *The Aesthetics of Pornography* by Peter Michelson contain between them the entire body of critical response to modern erotic writing. The other useful books in the area of criticism—*Sex in Literature* (1970) by John Atkins, *Eros Denied* (1964) by Wayland Young, *Pornography and the Law* (1959) by Eberhard and Phyllis Kronhausen, and *The Other Victorians* (1964) by Steven Marcus—either do not deal with modern erotic writing or they approach it from psychological, sociological, or legal perspectives. It is left to the reader to decide whether or not the writing discussed in this book merits further critical attention, but certainly it is plain that there has been very little of it.

Earlier we noted the categories into which erotic fiction falls, and discussed the inadequate hard-core and soft-core categorizations advanced by Michelson and the Kronhausens. These groupings are useful and convenient when applied in moderation, because they acknowledge that making distinctions is not only possible but necessary in a field that has too often been the victim of blanket condemnation. The outlines of critical theory Strother Purdy talks about begin in such categories, but the categories should be as simple and concise as possible, and free of the quasi-legal influence found in four-letter words like hard-core and soft-core. (The distinction between "hard" and "soft" is not much more meaningful than making a count of the number of Anglo-Saxon words on a page.)

Bearing in mind the definition of erotic literature as imaginative writing that is chiefly about sexuality, we can begin to discern the categories of the genre. All genre fiction begins with a formula of one kind or another. By definition genre novels are written within certain boundaries made necessary by their subject matter, while general fiction recognizes no such limitations. (*Crime and Punishment,* for example, shares many of the attributes of the detective novel, but is not genre fiction because Dostoevsky felt free to ignore the demands of that kind of story when they got in his way.) These limitations are imposed upon the author by his subject or his publisher, and the category his work falls into is determined by his resistance to and transformation of these formulas.

The masterpieces of erotic literature make up its highest and smallest category, of course, books whose content is dictated by the author's imagination rather than by the demands of his audience. Some of the novels in this category are *Story of O, Irene, Lolita, The Story of the Eye* and *The Real Thing.* In the second category are found novels in which the boundaries of the genre are expanded and transformed by the seriousness and originality of writers who utilize its conventions—somewhat like the poet's use of rhyme —for their own purposes. Most of the novels published by The Olympia Press and Essex House demonstrate the possibilities within this category. Finally, in the third and lowest category, we find novels so slavishly written to formula that we find in their impersonality no trace of the author. It is this last category—the largest—that has obscured the accomplishments made within the first two categories, and attracted the wrath of the censor as well as the contempt of literary critics. All that is left to say on this subject can be summed up by a description of the conventions of erotic fiction—the formula followed by writers in the third category. This formula is simply sex, sex, and more sex, divorced from the requirements of theme or characterization or plausible reality. Above all, what must be stressed about these formula novels is that they lie about the nature of sexuality. They ignore the spiritual basis of eroticism in order to capitalize on its animality, heedless that true eroticism flowers in the interaction of spirit and flesh.

These three categories of erotic literature partake of different modes: the assaultive, the seductive, and the philosophical. These terms refer to the effect erotic writing has on the reader; they seem infinitely more useful than older terms taken from legal, rather than literary, usage such as obscene, pornographic, or even emetic (Judge Woolsey's description of James Joyce's *Ulysses* in his decision admitting it into the United States).

The assaultive mode of erotic writing involves the extreme expression of the anarchic impulse in eroticism. Its aggressive, brutal images are designed to shock the reader into an awareness of the destructive, usually repressed aspect of his own erotic feelings. Apollinaire's *The Debauched Hospodar* and most of Sade's writings are deliberately assaultive. In a sense, the function of these books is therapeutic. They reassure the reader that his own assaultive feelings are not limited to him alone, and provide a catharsis seldom found outside of erotic literature.

The seductive and philosophical modes of erotic writing attempt to persuade the reader of the importance of eros by descriptive and intellectual means. In the seductive mode, an interesting story, believable characters, and vivid descriptions of erotic activity all work to seduce the reader into having a sympathetic response to the work. The significance of this response lies in his acceptance of erotic writing as a mirror reflecting his own erotic nature. The seductive mode must stimulate a sexual response, which is not necessarily true of the philosophical mode; here the object is to arouse a more complex set of responses that are as much intellectual as erotic. In the philosophical mode erotic feelings are stimulated in order to illustrate ideas about the nature of eroticism. Most of the masterpieces of erotic writing have been written in the philosophical mode, perhaps because the subject of eroticism lends itself to speculation about the nature of existence; but this is not to say that fiction written in the assaultive or seductive modes is devoid of ideas.

We have seen that erotic literature is capable of exploring and adapting to its subject most of the themes found in general literature, but there are two which recur again and again. An understanding of both is essential to an appreciation of erotic writing as literary art. The first of these themes involves a recognition of the importance of sexuality in human life beyond its reproductive function; the recognition that like it or not, we are ruled by eros equally as much as by the struggle for survival and fulfillment, and the awareness of death. This is the basic assumption of erotic literature, and perhaps the unacknowledged issue in every censorship case, for the censor is a person who denies the literary expression of eroticism in order to avoid confronting the truth of this assumption. If sexuality is not talked about or written about, then the questions it raises about the nature of man can be ignored. Pandora's box is better left shut, censors believe, and they can hardly be blamed for their caution, considering the psychic chaos treated in erotic fiction. It *is* frightening, but it is even more frightening when it is left unacknowledged. Dionysus gagged and buried is a destructive god.

It may be that people who accept in theory the importance of sexuality (when they read about it in the writings of Freud, Norman O. Brown, or any of the dozens of thinkers and poets since William Blake who have stressed its prominence in our lives) find it difficult to accept the imaginative pursuance of these theories in particular erotic novels. Yet that the one follows from the other, that there is a connection between the theory and its expression in erotic writing, is beyond dispute. There is a paragraph in Norman O. Brown's *Love's Body* (1966) referring to a passage in Blake which defines the nature of this connection.

> To return the word to the flesh. To make knowledge carnal again; not by deduction, but immediate by perception or sense at once; the bodily senses.

Let us follow this concise description of the highest function of erotic literature with one more quotation from Brown, in which he points to the second most important theme of erotic writing: the idea that the transcendence of self through eroticism is one of the ways by which we become privy to the unity of existence.

> Dionysus, the mad god, breaks down the boundaries; releases the prisoners; abolishes repression; and abolishes the *principium individuationis,* substituting for it the unity of man and the unity of man with nature. . . .

This is the central theme of erotic literature. It recurs again and again in the writing discussed in this book, and will be found somewhere in most good erotic novels, if not by direct statement, then by implication. It is a theme as old in the East as Taoism, whose teachers stressed the importance of sexual intercourse as a way for man and woman to transcend their individual egos and achieve union with existence; a theme as old in the West as Dionysus, and as current as Brown's interpretations of Freud. It is one of the underlying messages of poetry: during certain heightened moments of our lives, moments recreated in poems, the veil between our individual egos and the unity of all creation is lifted, and we are able to perceive the oneness of things, the design of existence.

Like poets, erotic writers attempt to recreate a heightened moment, that which may occur during sexual union. It is an experience shared by all humanity, the most democratic of all heightened moments except for death.

The essential unity of existence is the underlying principle of most of man's religious and philosophical thought; its appearance in the history of erotic literature attests to the hold it has on the human mind. Erotic writing in its highest form is the expression of this theme as it pertains to sexual experience, a secret record of the role played by eroticism in human life.

NOTE

EROTIC LITERATURE IS unexplored territory for most people, and no less so for bibliographers. Scholars have barely begun to set things tidy by assembling a complete bibliography in the field. Although the following bibliography is limited to some of the books referred to in this work, it does contain, in addition to lists of selected general, critical, and historical volumes, the first comprehensive listing of the significant books of modern erotic literature. With an eye to assisting scholars of the future I have tried where possible to note the date when a book was first published, although in many cases I had to settle for the date of the first American edition. Assembling this information is made difficult by the tendency of erotic writers to publish under pseudonyms, so I have noted the real names of authors wherever possible.

For a number of reasons I would like to express my thanks to Ed Sanders, Jerrold Mundis, John Brockman, and *Screw* magazine; most of all, however, to my wife Joyce.

SELECTED BIBLIOGRAPHY

I. General and Critical

Ashbee, Henry Spencer, *Index Librorum Prohibitorum or A Complete Guide to Forbidden Books,* London, 1877, North Hollywood, 1966.

Atkins, John, *Sex in Literature,* London, 1970.

Bataille, Georges, *L'érotisme, or Death And Sensuality,* Paris, 1957, New York, 1962, 1969.

Brown, Norman O., *Love's Body,* New York, 1966, 1968.

Buchen, Irving, editor; *The Perverse Imagination, Sexuality and Literary Culture,* New York, 1970.

Craig, Alec, *Suppressed Books, A History of the Conception of Literary Obscenity,* New York, 1963.

d'Arcangelo, Angelo, *The Homosexual Handbook,* New York, 1969.

d'Arcangelo, Angelo, *Angelo D'Arcangelo's Love Book: Inside the Sexual Revolution,* New York, 1971.

Hurwood, Bernhardt J., *The Golden Age of Erotica,* New York, 1968.

Kronhausen, Drs. Eberhard and Phyllis, *Pornography and the Law,* New York, 1959, 1964.

Loth, David, *The Erotic in Literature,* New York, 1961.

Marcus, Steven, *The Other Victorians,* New York, 1966.

Michelson, Peter, *The Aesthetics of Pornography,* New York, 1971.

Vassi, Marco, *The Stoned Apocalypse,* New York, 1972.

Vassi, Marco, *Metasex, Mirth & Madness,* New York, 1975.

Young, Wayland, *Eros Denied,* New York, 1964.

II. Historical

Anonymous, *My Secret Life,* New York, 1966.

Anon., *The Memoirs of Dolly Morton,* No. Hollywood, 1968.

Anon., *Flossie, A Venus of Fifteen*, Atlanta, Georgia, 1967.

Anon., *Autobiography of a Flea.*

Anon., *Rosa Fielding or The Victim of Lust*, No. Hollywood, 1968.

Anon., *The Love Pagoda*, No. Hollywood, 1965.

Anon., *The Lustful Turk*, New York, 1967.

Anon., *Randiana, or Excitable Tales*, No. Hollywood, 1967.

Chorier, Nicolas, *The Dialogues of Luisa Sigea*, No. Hollywood, 1965.

Cleland, John, *Memoirs of a Woman of Pleasure*, New York, 1963.

Crébillon Le Fils, *A Lady of Quality*, No. Hollywood, 1964.

Devereaux, Captain Charles, *Venus in India*, Los Angeles, 1967.

Douglas, Norman, *Some Limericks*, New York, 1967.

Hall, J. Mortimer, *The Unexpurgated Anecdota Americana*, in two volumes, No. Hollywood, 1968.

Herbert, Lord George, *A Night in a Moorish Harem*, No. Hollywood, 1967.

Li Yü, *Jou Pou Tuan*, New York, 1963.

Sade, Donatien Alphonse François, Marquis de, *The Complete Justine, Philosophy in the Bedroom, And Other Writings*, New York, 1965.

Sade, D. A. F., *The 120 Days of Sodom*, New York, 1966.

Sade, D. A. F., *Juliette*, New York, 1968.

Wilmot, John, Earl of Rochester, *Sodom, or The Quintessence of Debauchery*, No. Hollywood, 1966.

III. Modern Erotic Literature

(Because of the importance of two publishers in this field, Essex House in North Hollywood, California, and The Olympia Press in New York, I have chosen to divide this section of the bibliography into three parts: novels published by The Olympia Press in New York, by Essex House, and by other publishers.

A. The Olympia Press in New York

Amory, Richard, *Frost*, 1973.

Auden, Renee, *The Party*, 1971.

——————, *High Thrust*, 1972.
Barrows, Philip, *Whores, Queers and Others*, two volumes.
Daimler, Harriet, *The Organization*, 1968.
——————, *The Woman Thing*, 1973.
——————, *Innocence*, 1968.
——————, *Darling*, 1973.
D'Arcangelo, Angelo, *Sookey*, 1969.
di Prima, Diane, *Memoirs of a Beatnik*, 1969.
Durand, Orson, *Angel in the Flesh*, 1969.
Girodias, Maurice, *The New Olympia Reader*, 1970.
Harris, Merril, *Dirty Alice*, 1970.
Horn, Jon, *Doctor Onan*, 1970.
——————, *Bondage Trash*, 1968.
Kimball, George, *Only Skin Deep*, 1968.
Lemercier, Juliette and Justine, *The Turkish Bath*, 1969.
Kung, Tor, *My Mother Taught Me*, 1963, 1968.
——————, *Forever Ecstasy*, 1968.
Major, Clarence, *All-Night Visitors*, 1969.
Malzberg, Barry, *Oracle of the Thousand Hands*, 1968.
——————, *Screen*, 1968.
——————, *In My Parents' Bedroom*, 1971.
Martin, Ed, *Busy Bodies*, 1963, 1968.
——————, *The Masterpiece*, 1969.
——————, *Inch by Inch*, 1968.
——————, *Frankenstein '69*, 1969.
Moore, Robert, *The Rape Conspiracy*, 1971.
——————, *Lady Killer*, 1969.
Newman, Frank, *Barbara*, 1968.
Peachum, Thomas, *The Watcher and the Watched*, 1955, 1967.
Peckinpah, Deneen, *Ceremonies of Love*, 1970.
Piombo, Akbar Del, *The Erotic Tool*, 1971.
——————, *Into the Harem*, 1970.
——————, *Cosimo's Wife*, 1955, 1967.
——————, *Who Pushed Paula?*, 1955, 1967.
——————, *The Double-Bellied Companion*, 1955, 1967.
Reck, Alexander, *Colors Roar By*, 1969.
Sage, Jett, *Crazy Wild*, 1968.
——————, *Crazy Wild Breaks Loose*, 1968.
Sativa, Mary, *Acid Temple Ball*, 1971.
——————, *The Lovers' Crusade*, 1971.
Seftali, Lela, *Ride A Cock-Horse*, 1970.

Solomita, Stephen, *Victoria Welles,* 1969.
Tavel, Ronald, *Street of Stairs,* 1968.
Townsend, Larry, *Run, Little Leather Boy,* 1971.
Vanden, Dirk, *I Want It All,* 1970.
—————————, *All or Nothing,* 1971.
—————————, *All Is Well,* 1971.
Vanek, C. S., *The Skin Book,* 1969.
—————————, *Hide and Sex,* 1969.
Vassi, Marco, *Mind Blower,* 1970.
—————————, *The Saline Solution,* 1971.
—————————, *The Gentle Degenerates,* 1970.
—————————, *Contours of Darkness,* 1972.
Walbrook, Louise, *The Demon's Feast (Gordon),* 1966, 1968.
Warfield, Selena, *The Whip Angels,* 1955, 1968.
Watson, J., *The Sexual Adventures of Sherlock Holmes,* 1971.
Winter, Anna, *Flesh and Blood,* 1969.

B. Essex House

Anderson, Jerry, *Trans,* 1969.
Bradbrook, Gary, *Get It On!,* 1969.
Bukowski, Charles, *Notes of a Dirty Old Man,* 1969.
Dallas, Paul V., *Binding With Briars,* 1968.
Dedeaux, P. N., *Tender Buns,* 1969.
—————————, *The Nothing Things,* 1969.
Doyle, Kirby, *Happiness Bastard,* 1968.
Farmer, Philip José, *The Image of the Beast,* 1968.
—————————, *Blown,* 1969.
—————————, *A Feast Unknown,* 1969.
Gallion, Jane, *Stoned,* 1969.
—————————, *Biker,* 1969.
Geis, Richard E., *Raw Meat,* 1969.
—————————, *Ravished,* 1968.
Lamont, Gil, *Roach,* 1969.
Luck, Barry, *Gropie,* 1969.
Marlowe, Alan S., *Over Easy,* 1969.
MacPherson, Michael, *Abducted,* 1968.
McNaughton, Jr., Charles, *Mindblower,* 1969.
Meltzer, David, *The Agency,* 1968.
—————————, *The Agent,* 1968.
—————————, *How Many Blocks in the Pile?,* 1968.

—————, *Orf*, 1968.
—————, *The Martyr*, 1969.
—————, *Lovely*, 1969.
—————, *Healer*, 1969.
—————, *Out*, 1969.
—————, *Glue Factory*, 1969.
Perkins, Michael, *Blue Movie*, 1968.
—————, *Evil Companions*, 1968.
—————, *Queen of Heat*, 1968.
—————, *The Tour*, 1969.
—————, *Whacking Off*, 1969.
—————, *Terminus*, 1969.
—————, *Estelle*, 1969.
—————, *Down Here*, 1970.
Porter, Gil, *Coupled*, 1968.
Ramirez, Alice Louise, *The Geek*, 1969.
Stine, Hank, *Season of the Witch*, 1968.
—————, *Thrill City*, 1969.
Toledano, Henry, *The Bitter Seed*, 1969.
—————, *A Sort of Justice*, 1969.

C. Other Publishers

Anonymous, *M. Fontaine's Establishment*, New York, 1969.
Amory, Richard, *Loon Song*, New York, 1968.
—————, *Willow Song*, New York, 1974.
Apollinaire, Guillaume, *The Debauched Hospodar* and *Memoirs Of A Young Rakehell*, Paris, 1959.
Arsan, Emmanuelle, *Emmanuelle*, New York, 1971.
—————, *Emmanuelle II*, New York, 1974.
Bataille, Georges, *The Story of the Eye* and *The Naked Beast at Heaven's Gate*, No. Hollywood, 1968.
—————, *The Little One*, in the magazine *Living Hand 1*, Paris, 1973.
Berg, Jean de, *The Image*, New York, 1966.
Blasi, Raphael, *Private Boy (Nothing To It)*, New York, 1975.
Daimler, Harriet, *The Woman Thing*, No. Hollywood, 1967.
—————, *Darling*, No. Hollywood, 1967.
————— with Henry Crannach, *The Pleasure Thieves*, San Diego, 1968.
Delany, Samuel R., *The Tides of Lust*, New York, 1973.

Drake, Hamilton, *Sin for Breakfast*, No. Hollywood, 1967.

Ford, Charles Henri, and Parker Tyler, *The Young and Evil*, Paris, 1933, 1960.

Genet, Jean, *Our Lady of the Flowers*, New York, 1963.

—————, *The Thief's Journal*, New York, 1964.

—————, *Miracle of the Rose*, New York, 1966.

—————, *Funeral Rites*, New York, 1969.

—————, *Querelle of Breast*, London, 1966.

Girodias, Maurice, editor, *The Olympia Reader*, New York, 1965.

—————, editor, *The New Olympia Reader*, New York, 1970.

Hayim, George, *Obsession*, New York, 1970.

Heller, Marcus van, *The Loins of Amon*, No. Hollywood, 1967.

—————, *The Wantons*, No. Hollywood, 1967.

—————, *The House of Borgia*, No. Hollywood, 1967.

—————, *Kidnap*, No. Hollywood, 1967.

—————, *Nightmare*, No. Hollywood, 1967.

—————, *Cruel Lips*, No. Hollywood, 1967.

—————, *Roman Orgy*, No. Hollywood, 1966.

—————, *Rape*, No. Hollywood, 1967.

—————, *Adam and Eve*, Covina, California, 1967.

—————, *Terror*, Covina, California, 1967.

Hitt, Orrie, *Hotel Woman*, New York, 1959.

Jones, Henry, *The Enormous Bed*, No. Hollywood, 1967.

Kaye, H. R., *The Maid*, No. Hollywood, 1968.

Klossowski, Pierre, *Roberte Ce Soir & The Revolution of the Edict of Nantes*, New York, 1969.

Lawrence, D. H., *Lady Chatterley's Lover*, New York, 1959.

Lawton, Jeff, *Screw 22*, San Diego, 1969.

Louÿs, Pierre, *Mother's Three Daughters*, New York, 1969.

—————, *Aphrodite*, privately printed, 1925.

Lovin, Roger, *Eleven*, No. Hollywood, 1970.

McClure, Michael, *The Mad Club*, New York, 1970.

Meltzer, David, *Star*, No. Hollywood, 1970.

Miller, Henry, *Tropic of Cancer*, Paris, 1934.

—————, *Tropic of Capricorn*, Paris, 1937, 1938.

—————, *Black Spring*, New York, 1963.

—————, *Sexus*, Paris, 1962.

Mardaan, Ataullah, *Deva Dasi*, No. Hollywood, 1967.

—————, *Kama Houri*, No. Hollywood, 1967.

Nabokov, Vladimir, *Lolita,* New York, 1955.
Perez, Faustino, *Until She Screams,* No. Hollywood, 1967.
Réage, Pauline, *Story of O,* New York, 1965.
——————, *Return to the Chateau,* New York, 1971.
Routisie, Albert de, *Irene,* New York, 1969.
Sherwood, James, *Stradella,* Paris, 1962.
Skir, Leo, *Boychick,* New York, 1971.
Spade, Malcolm, *The Dealer,* No. Hollywood, 1970.
Talsman, William, *The Gaudy Image,* Paris, 1958.
Trocchi, Alexander, *Young Adam,* London, 1966.
——————, *Helen and Desire,* No. Hollywood, 1967.
——————, *The Carnal Days of Helen Seferis,* No. Hollywood, 1967.
——————, *White Thighs,* No. Hollywood, 1967.
——————, *Thongs,* No. Hollywood, 1967.
——————, *School for Wives,* No. Hollywood, 1967.
Vassi, Marco, *The French Job,* New York, 1973.
——————, *Pro Ball Groupie,* New York, 1974.
——————, *In Touch,* New York, 1975.
Wilde, Oscar, *Teleny, or the Reverse of the Medal,* No. Hollywood, 1967.

INDEX OF AUTHORS

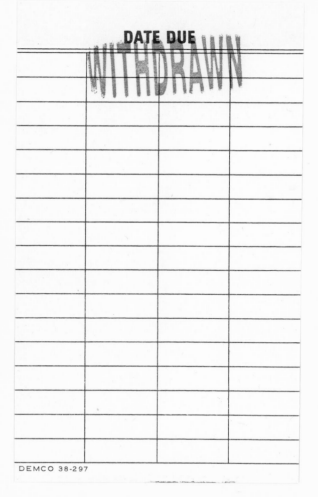

DATE DUE

WITHDRAWN